Everyone's Guid

Everyone's Guide to the Hereafter

Ken Akehurst
*The blind medium who passed to the
Higher Life on 28 July 1978*

Transmitted by G. M. Roberts

The C. W. Daniel Company Limited
1 Church Path, Saffron Walden,
Essex CB10 1JP

Published in Great Britain in 1985 by
The C. W. Daniel Co., Ltd.,
1 Church Path, Saffron Walden,
Essex CB10 1JP

Reprinted 1991

© G.M. Roberts 1981
ISBN 0 85435 414 X

Printed and bound by
Hillman Printers (Frome) Ltd,
Somerset

To my dear friends, Hilda and Dickie, without whom
this book would not have been possible.

About the Author

My husband was born on the 14th April, 1916 and christened Kennith Aylmer.

His health was not good from the beginning and the reason why he did not start school at the age most children do. In fact he was ten years old when he attended Brondesbury College. Later he took a secretarial course at Pitman's College in London.

His keen interest in motor cars led him to become an apprentice to the Sunbeam Talbot company where he eventually became a test driver.

Later he joined de Havilland where he was secretary to the Designer of Light Aircraft. He was with them for 14 years.

He moved to I.C.I. in Welwyn Garden City and was with them for 18 years. It was during this time that he found interest in spiritualism and became an enthusiastic Member of the Church.

By August 1971 we had moved to Eastbourne. It was at this time that the diabetes, that had plagued him for most of his life, caused him to lose his sight. Almost at the same time his psychic powers developed considerably, as did his healing.

Much more can be said about my husband but I think he will be remembered as much as anything for his genuine wish to help people, whenever he could. It does not surprise me, therefore, that he would have wanted to write this book. That, and his style of writing, convince me that it is indeed my husband who is author of this book.

Marjorie Akehurst,
Eastbourne.

Foreword

I have known Ken Akehurst and his wife intimately for a very long time. Ken was in my developing circle, for a while, before he went completely blind. I had to stand by and watch the great trauma that Ken and Marjorie went through, during the onset of the blindness. He returned to my circle to complete the development of his mediumship, which he did very rapidly. I would have recommended him anywhere as a very good medium, but unfortunately his health prevented him from travelling.

I have no hesitation in saying that I can hear Ken speak through the pages of this book, so many of his expressions and phrases. I have no doubt in my mind that Ken is the author of this book and that his words will be of great comfort and help to all who read it.

Gladys Fieldhouse,
M.S.A.G.B.
Eastbourne.

Chapter 1

When the time comes for us to pass over, one of several things happen. You are either met by someone known to you assuming your passing is normal, or, if not, then by someone who is appointed to do so. Do not worry about this for, whichever way it happens, it will seem perfectly all right at the time.

The normal passing does not have to be in bed, it can happen at any time that is right for you. Just remember you will be met. You do not arrive and find yourself lost. You are shown every step of the way. Those who pass over as a result of an accident or are killed by others are taken by helpers to a Centre where they are helped to understand what has happened. You see, the normal passing is planned and each and every one knows what is to happen. All your friends over here know and will be there to greet you. It is a happy occasion and you will be surprised how many friends you have, happy that you have made the crossing and are now safe forever in this wonderful World of Spirit.

You cannot begin to understand what it is like here; it is so much better than anything you have ever imagined. But I stray from what I have to tell you.

When you first arrive you feel, naturally, very strange. You have lost your Earth body and with it all the things that you have had wrong with you. Gone are all your aches and pains! If you are blind, as I was, you can see again and that, as you can believe, is a wonderful thing. I went round to all my friends, on Earth, to see what they looked like, for a start! Once you have got used to this new way of life you find there are so many things to do. You can go to school to find out more about life here or you can tackle other things, such as helping people who are over here but are not as far advanced as yourself. This may sound odd but on the Earth Plane we all develop in different ways, so that when we arrive here we have a different understanding of what this new life is about.

It matters quite a lot how advanced you are when you arrive, for all you have then is your true self, nothing to hide your true self behind, such as position in life, money or life style. What you are you are and plain for everyone to see. This should be kept in mind by all who think of nothing but themselves. Do not think that you change in the slightest when you arrive here, all you have lost is your Earthly body. If you have led what is known as a good life then you have nothing to fear. Most people pass through life having done things that they would rather forget about and they can, for there is no real evil in them. But for those who have been really evil, they must pay for it before they may join normal society in this life. Remember that there is perfect Justice over here. Not the Justice of the Earth Plane where society takes revenge. No. It is Justice tempered with Love. In fact, it is love that controls this life over here. If you do not have love in your heart, then life is very different. fortunately, for most of us, we have more of this love than we think, so that when we arrive we respond to all the love we are given and, in this way, the best in us comes out. On the other hand the worst may come out of some and it is here that help is needed and given.

You now have to consider what you are going to do about preparing yourself, for this new life. There is much that you have been told that is not right. You have been told that there is a Heaven and a Hell. There are no such places. When you arrive you go to the area where you are most suited, where you feel most at home. When you think of it, this is the most natural thing to do. On the Earth Plane, given the choice, you will always go to the places you like and mix with the people you like and feel at home with. Well, what is so strange about doing that over here? It is also natural that all your friends and loved ones are living in the same area. When you arrive, depending on your passing, you will either have a period of rest or some other kind of rehabilitation. Nothing is asked of you. When you are spiritually fit and well then you yourself will decide what you want to do. Naturally there are plenty of helpers around to set you off on the right path. They do this with Love and they really want you to progress. That is the wonderful thing about being 'dead'! People really do have your best interest at heart. There is no jealousy. People rejoice at the success of others. On the Earth Plane you have people who like nothing better than to see the other person make a mess of things, for that gives them satisfaction. Over here it is the other way round. All work to help the other succeed. But, you say, I thought you said we arrive, in spirit, just as we are but without our Earth bodies. Well, this is so, but what you must keep in mind is the fact that you go to the area that is best for you and therefore you are among your own kind who only want you to succeed. On the Earth Plane you are all together, like and unlike together, and you are not so free in your choice.

Now this is where you can help yourself prepare for this New Life. You are given a free choice on the Earth Plane to make what you will of life. You know this to be so. It does not matter, at all, about your station in life, you are always given the choice as to how you live it. It is not for me to tell you how you should behave, you know this yourself. All I say is that it is how you chose to live that decides when you arrive the area into which you will go. Think about this and you will see the perfect logic of it. You are in Heaven or Hell but in a state of your own making and, therefore choice. Does this seem odd to you? It should not. On the Earth Plane you say like attracts like. Well, so it does here. On the Earth you hear people say that they want to better themselves or they know of someone who has. On this side of life it is the same. People arrive here and after a time, when they have settled down, they start to look to see how they can improve themselves. it is then that they are given all the help they need. If, on the other hand, they are happy with their lot they are left alone. No pressure is put upon them. The reason for people, over here, wanting to advance is Spiritual, on the Earth Plane it is material. Therein lies the difference.

Do not run away with the idea that anything you have done on the Earth Plane that is evil will be overlooked. It will not, and you will have to answer for it. But you will answer by putting it right yourself. You will want to do this so that you may advance in this life. If I make this sound easy, I have to tell you that it is not. You have got to make amends for the wrong you have done. This, you will understand, can take many forms. But the big thing to remember is that it is just and for your own Spiritual good. Not a matter of taking revenge, as I have said before. If you have behaved well on the Earth Plane, then you are saved all this. In fact, this is what this Book is about, making sure that you come over here in the best possible shape.

When I was on the Earth Plane I lived a normal kind of life. I would drink too much at times and certainly smoked too much; but there is nothing wrong in this so far as this life is concerned. It is just that you arrive, over here, with the habit or desire and there is no way you can satisfy it. So my advice is to give up both if you can before you come over. I did not drink towards the end because I was diabetic, but I did smoke as I say, too much, and I really am having to pay for that, even

3

now after a year. Sex is another thing. Usually by the end of one's life this is under control. Yet I have met quite a few people, over here, who are having a bad time because they did not get this part of their life properly organised. The lesson is to be moderate in all things, which also goes for eating. So that when you arrive, over here, where all those things do not exist, you can soon manage without them.

I have been asked to tell you, by my advisers, that all the bad habits of the Earth Plane come over with you and to start with they can make your life difficult. Such as your thoughts and language. On the Earth Plane the former cannot be picked up, and your language you can usually get away with. Over here, what you think is plain for all to hear and bad language gives offence, so, for your own good, try to keep these matters fit for all to hear.

Do you ever stop to think what it would be like if you just let your thoughts and your actions have a free rein? You could not do it long on the Earth Plane, you would be locked up. Over here you can, there is no one to stop you, you have free will. Now the point I am trying to make is this. When you are on the Earth Plane learn to control yourself so that you really can handle this new way of living and make your quality of life here that much better from the start. You know, even today on the Earth Plane, good manners are appreciated. Well they are over here, only more so.

You will now have to consider the question of having to live without your Earth body. To begin with it is very strange. You have had a body for quite a long time, usually and you miss it. The first thing to remember is that people over here can see you for exactly what you are. Gone are the things that made up yourself on the Earth Plane. You are now your true self. This does not pose much of a problem. If your life has been a reasonable one, but if it has not been it is not so easy. There are different colours for different states of Spiritual health and these colours make up the clothes you wear over here, so you see, you cannot hide your true self at all. This is the reason why you should try to come over, as fit as you can Spiritually. If you think you can change things in the last few years, you cannot. It is the way you have lived all your life that decides the colours for they are forming all the time, as you live. The good things and the bad go together to make up the shades which will then be your spirit clothes when you arrive.

The good news is that the colours can be changed by your efforts over here and this is the true base of Spirit life and why there is hope for

4

all, no matter how much of a sinner you are when you arrive. I cannot stress this too greatly for it is a very big shock to some people when they arrive and find that things are not the way they thought or as they had been led to believe by people who should know better. Even after many years in the Spiritualist Movement I had not been properly prepared for this life and that is why I am writing this book, so that you, the reader, and others, if you will pass the word along, may be better prepared than myself and many like me. If I can prevent some of the suffering I have seen in others, since I have been here, then I will be doing much good.

Chapter 2

I am now going to talk about passing into Spirit in some detail. First the normal way which is, despite what you may think, the usual way for most of us.

Your passing has been arranged by powers beyond our understanding and all interested parties are notified. Then the person chosen to bring you home will arrive at your side and say, as my sister did 'Come on, you have had enough of this' and away you will go. No one I have spoken to has asked to be allowed to stay a little longer! The one chosen to fetch you is always a loved one so you have no fear about going with them. The next thing to remember is that there is absolutely no pain attached to the business of passing. You may be in pain from whatever is the matter with you but if you are in no pain then you will feel nothing. In my case I was listening to the Test match England v New Zealand on July 28th 1978, when my time came—even that did not hold me and I love cricket—and off I went with my sister. I did not even think to say goodbye to my wife who was in the kitchen preparing lunch. She who had looked after me so well all the years of my blindness and whom I loved and still do very much. Now have you taken the point I am trying to make. When the time comes you just drop everything and go with pleasure and without pain.

When you pass over you are being born again into this new world and you need to be looked after like a new born baby. First, depending upon your state of Spiritual Health, you are taken to a place of rest. This is necessary because of the change of environment from the Earth Plane to Spirit. There, depending upon your state, you are treated by Spirit doctors who will make you fit to start life here. They have so many wonderful things to use and they know what each soul needs. When you think of all the hit and miss treatment on the Earth Plane it makes you sad that doctors have such a poor opinion of Spirit Healing, but more about that later.

Now fit and ready to start our new life we need the help of friends to show us round and teach us, as new babies, how to carry on over here.

As we have free will, remember, they can only show us the paths open to us, they will not tell us what to do. This is the Law, advice is gladly given, help is freely given but orders NO!

Now let us talk about abnormal passing which is a very different kettle of fish. Here we have the situation where the Soul is not at all ready to be called home, in fact the poor one is not being called at all, but being sent. The difference is great and not looked upon with pleasure here at all. Especially is this so where Man has had a hand in it. The soul has had its education on the Earth Plane cut short, and so is not ready to take its place in the Life here and therefore cannot do so. They are in limbo and very hard to help. I am now talking about people who take their own lives or have their lives taken by others before their time. They do not know how to cope with the new position in which they find themselves and it is very hard for helpers to contact them. Remember they now have free will and anything they think of doing they can do. That is why it is so wrong for life to be taken in this way on the Earth Plane.

People who come over after a disaster such as famine or an air crash are in a different category, and are much easier to help from a spirit point of view. There are times, as in War, when the helpers here are hard pressed to cope, but in most cases they are able to reach the soul and explain what has happened. When they can do this it can be treated as a normal passing, for in a way it is. These are normal souls killed through no fault of their own, who need help, and so it is easy for it to be given. The same can be said for road accidents. Once the soul has accepted what has happened then help can be given, but the evil soul dispatched to this side by execution, is in a very bad state indeed and if Governments, who practice this kind of thing knew the trouble they cause the Spirit World and the soul concerned, I am sure they would stop it. You must remember that the Grand Design is to help each and every one, regardless of how evil, to advance to perfection in time and here lies the problem for us over here.

Then there is the case of drug taking. The poor soul that passes this way is in real trouble for not only has it taken its own life but it still has its craving for the drug. Naturally all efforts are made to help but the condition the soul is in makes it very difficult and distressing to those concerned. it will also be very distressing for those who have lost their loved ones through drugs. Please remember that the helpers never give up. They will succeed in the end, but how much better it would be if the drug had not been taken in the first place. If the poor one suffers in passing so do those who have supplied the drugs, for gain. So you can see it is in the best interest of all if drugs are left out of your way of life.

You will want to know why it is that some people pass over so young and others live to a fine old age. It is not easy to answer that for, as I have said before, the time for each passing is set by the Divine Power. The time on Earth is a time for learning and when the soul has had its lesson then it is time to pass over. Do you go back to Earth to lead another life if it is necessary? Frankly I do not know and although I have asked that question myself, over here, I cannot get an answer. My feeling is that you do not. The lessons on the Earth Plane are important but by spirit standards, very basic, and providing you have learned enough to be able to carry on here, as people seem to, then I cannot see why we should go back. The big idea is to advance.

Many people wonder why it is necessary for a baby to be born only to pass over after a short stay on Earth. All who have suffered this will ask why? Take comfort. The little one is taken good care of and, as in normal passing, goes willingly and without pain. It then grows up in the same way as it would on the Earth Plane. The big difference being that it is growing up in Spirit. They naturally become advanced spirits much faster and that is the object of the exercise, but it was necessary for them to start from the Earth Plane. Do not fear, you will see them again, when the time is right. But if you could see these spirit children playing and living together it would do your heart good. Such happiness has never been seen on Earth. They remember you and love you. All we ask is that you go on loving them and be happy for them that they are leading such wonderful lives.

Now, about your pets. the first thing to say is that as they all have souls, they pass into spirit like the rest of us. We have everything here just as you have on Earth. Jesus said that the time would come when the lion would lie down with the lamb. this is where it happens. Your pet, because you loved it, loves you, and this is the bond between us all which makes certain we meet again when the time comes. Do not fear, there are people over here who look after pets and make sure they settle down. There are people who love all animals and for this reason they do this job and do it well. If you could see your pet at play it would do your heart good. Like the rest of us it is young again and all its old ills have gone, left behind in its Earth body.

Do you ever think about all the poor animals that are killed for food. God created them for man to eat, but He did not expect that man would cause them such suffering in the process. We are all very grieved, over here, when we see the way these animals are treated. There is absolutely no reason or excuse for it. Cruelty of any kind is a sign of a base nature and will not do the owner much good over here. Farming today, in some cases, has taken a very bad turn for the worse. In the name of progress, some are causing great suffering. We speak about calves being taken from their mothers too early and then kept in a confined space so that, when the time comes for them to leave, they find it difficult to walk. Then the way they are fed causes them suffering. Powdered milk is not what they need and man knows it. Let me tell you this, all suffering is bad. Bad for the sufferer and bad for the soul of he who causes the suffering and it does not matter to whom or what. The soul causing all this suffering must pay for it in order to be returned to normal health. Do not cause suffering to man or beast is our best advice to you for it must be paid for. There are plenty of people over here who wish they had taken this advice. I have taken one example, the calf, but much suffering is caused to all creatures used for food, and this is bad for those causing it and society as a whole. Your Government must be made to know that the people will not stand for it and strict laws must be passed to have it stopped. I cannot reiterate it strongly enough, suffering in any form, is an evil and those who cause it will realise it when the time comes to leave the body. The colour of their spirit body will not be a pleasant sight. My advice to you is to do all you can to have it stopped. You have the R.S.P.C.A. as your first step. Support them, they are doing a good job, and we know it.

After looking at Man's base nature it is nice to be able to turn to happier things. It is indeed fortunate that the base ones do not make up the majority. Now we turn to those who find it easier to be kind than cruel. Their souls, during their life time, attain a colour that is most pleasing to the spirit eye and it is they who are able to move about here with most confidence. They are the lucky ones. It is easy for them because it is natural for them so to do. Then there are those who are not kind by nature but who know it is right. They have to work at it and, if successful, they too attain a colour that is pleasing. The point I want to make is that however you are made, providing your heart is in the right place, as they say, and you do good along your way through life, your reward will be the colour of your soul when you pass on.

Some people have time to do good and can go out and do it. Others, like the busy housewife, cannot. This does not matter. What matters is that you give the help you can when it is needed and do not 'hurry by, on the other side of the road'.

You may think that I am not being very helpful when I say these things, but I am. You do not have to run round doing good to obtain the desired colour of your soul. It comes by having the right thoughts. If you do acts of charity only for appearances sake that will get you precisely nowhere. It is the thought behind it, that is important. Take the person who does Meals on Wheels. If they are doing it to impress others, then they may succeed, but that is all, they are not doing it with love in their hearts for the people they serve. If, on the other hand, they do this worthwhile job because they truly wish to help, then they are doing themselves some good at the same time. Have I made my point? The thought is the spiritual part of all acts of charity and therefore if the thought is not a loving one then the act is as nothing. Will the people on the Earth Plane ever get this right?

Those of us who know the truth of this want to help you not to make the same mistake. If we can help you we are also helping ourselves. When money is given to anyone or anything and it is not given in the right way, then it is as nothing to the giver. The person who receives it, or the charity, are pleased enough but we are talking about the job of having your soul the right colour when you arrive over here and nothing else. If the idea is to do this then you need all the help you can get and this is the reason for all I have said in this book. If we can help you, and we do it with love, we will help ourselves, also.

Chapter 3

We have talked about the act of passing. The next step is to tell you of all the loving care that is taken of you after you arrive. I have suggested that you are, at the start, as a little baby. There are Homes of Rest for the weary traveller from the Earth Plane and believe me you are weary to begin with. How am I to describe these Homes? It is difficult to describe the World of Spirit so that you, on the Earth Plane can understand and, more important, believe? If you do not believe what we are telling you then our time is wasted, for the only reason for writing is to help. For your own good please believe what you read here.

To proceed. The Home of Rest is built of a kind of marble with the most wonderful colours running through it. There are many of these Homes but they all follow a pattern. Colour is everywhere, for it plays a big part in spirit healing and the colours themselves are so different from those of the Earth Plane. You see the rainbow, the sunset or sunrise and you are impressed with the beauty but the colour over here is always so much softer, with so many tints, and always with light in it. Colours run into each other, so soft, in fact the only word is spiritual, and all this soft light and colour is used to restore the soul to strength. Also sleep. The soul is usually very tired when it arrives so it is put to bed as it were. You must remember that, in this world, the temperature is always the same. In fact there s no temperature but it is the only way I can make you understand. The atmosphere is perfect and therefore the weary soul can rest without covering and on something more like a couch than a bed. Each soul has a room to itself and I can hear you saying 'what is it like?' I will do my best to describe it. It is not very large and there is only the couch in it. The ceiling, walls and floor are all of the same beautiful marble, with all this delicate colouring. There is a doorway but no door, rather a kind of muslin drape and in the background lovely soft, sweet music.

The helpers are trained in the art of caring for the souls that are put in their charge and know how to find out the needs of each, for we are all suffering from different conditions of the soul, just as we have suffered different conditions of the body when on earth. The treatments, being of spirit, are mostly to do with vibrations, hence all the colour and the wonderful music. It is a pity more colour and music of the right kind are not used on Earth. Time, as you know it, does not mean anything here, there are no clocks and no calendars, so we cannot say how long each soul has in the home. Some need longer than others and you stay there only for as long as is necessary to make you fit. During the time you are there you sleep and are given treatment.

When you are ready to leave, your loved one, who is looking after you at the start of your spirit life, arrives, and away you go together. In my case my sister arrived and I went home to her place. I must explain a little more about the arrival of the soul over here. Most of us do not know what to expect when we arrive. Even myself, who had been in the Spiritualist Movement for so long, could not quite take it in, and again, what we are told does not measure up to reality. So you can understand that those who have had no spiritual education at all, or have had their heads filled with a lot of nonsense, will have problems. I was soon able to adjust and as I have always had an open mind this also helped, but so many arrive looking for St. Peter and the Gate. Others wait for judgment to be handed out, not knowing which way they are to go. I tell you they are in a state. It is all right to joke about it because, when they find out the truth, they are so happy. No harps, no haloes and no judgment as such, just peace and goodwill.

But there are those, and the Church on Earth must carry the blame, who cannot accept the reality of this life and it takes much love and spirit power to free them from the bonds their souls have been in over the years, through all kinds of false teaching. Herein lies the power of thought. On the Earth Plane thought is not given anything like the importance it should and certainly its power is not understood. This is a great pity for if a soul, for years and years, has been filled with thoughts about 'Heaven' then that is what is built up for them and they cannot face the truth. The other thing is the fact that, when you pass into spirit, you enter into a solid world and you are solid. It is the Earth Plane that becomes shadow. You must understand this, for it is very important. So you see, if you arrive expecting something that has been built up for you, and it is not so, then you are unable to accept and as free will also comes into it, this causes great difficulties.

12

Fortunately there are wonderful Spirit Leaders here who, over countless years, have discovered the correct way to put this matter right, but it is such a pity that a soul has to arrive in such a state. If only you, and all mankind, would accept the simple truth that there is no death and that your time on Earth is but a place of learning, whence the soul can make a start that will take it on and on from one state of development to the next. Ever improving until we know not what except it is God's wish for us and, as He loves us, it can only be for our good. But no, man carries on as if the Earth is the only place and that he must make the most of this life for that is all there is. Jesus came to Earth to explain that there is no death and went through trouble and suffering to prove it. He also taught that we should love one another and above all love God. He gave us a simple set of rules by which to live, and all this was aimed at giving us the chance to prepare our souls for the time when we should enter the World of Spirit. It is all very simple, but have our teachers done His bidding? When you see the state some souls arrive, the answer can only be no. This is not only a Christian failing, many wonderful teachers have visited the Earth Plane and have also failed.

Do not despair, there are many over here who were given the wrong advice as to how best to prepare for the Spirit World and who have been able to throw off the drawback and have come out of it well, but they all say how much easier it would have been if they had known the truth. They would have been saved a lot of worry on the Earth Plane and much hard work over here. What do I mean about all that? Simply this.

If you were told by your religious teachers that there is no death. That when you pass over you are just changing one way of life for another, then you would have a different approach to life on Earth. If you were told that you do not change at all when you pass, you just lose your Earth body, and gain an Astral one, then the chances are you would take more care of your soul and see that it is in good shape for your future life. But your teachers do not tell you this. They think there could be a life after death but what kind they are not going to tell us, for as they see it, no one has come back to say. They forget that Jesus did so. They think that people, like me, writing a book about it, are working for the devil. Nothing could be further from the truth. They are the ones who are going to have to answer, not those like me. Think for a moment, suppose you thought you would have a nice little chat about death with your friends how far do you think you would get? It is just not done, and why? Because you have been taught, and people before you, down through the ages, that death is about the last thing you want to have happen to you. Life on this Earth Plane is the place. This is where you have everything. You keep people alive who are very sick or very old. Where there is life there is hope, you say, and your doctors fight hard to keep people alive. They say that they must, they have taken an oath, but in so many cases they put the oath before the wellbeing of the patient. How different it would all be if your teachers could have known the truth about death and had told you, as I do now, that life goes on. That all the sick and suffering people you pray for, should look upon death as a friend. That you should talk about it, and prepare for it and get yourself into the best possible shape for it, so that your soul arrives in a condition that you and your friends can be proud of. The life you are leading now will decide the kind of clothes you arrive over here in. The colours in your soul will tell the story for all to see. So you can see, you and your friends over here are either going to be proud of you or perhaps somewhat ashamed. There are other degrees naturally, but you can see what I mean.

On earth, things have changed a bit, the smart thing is to look as if you are a tramp but to let it be known that it cost the earth. Not so over here and it never will be, you look just what you are. It is at this point that I must say again, all is not lost. If you really want to improve your soul, then you will receive all the help you need and it will be given in love, for that is the coin of our realm. On the Earth Plane, success is measured by money and position and this in turn, is demonstrated by possessions. This part you know only too well and it can all cause much unhappiness, can it not? Over here it is only the colour of your soul that matters. Now I am not saying that people should not try and get on, it is in one's nature and one strives for this over here and for ever. It is a driving force. Some have more than others but all have it. No, it is the way one sets about it that matters. You know, without me telling you, that it is wrong to make progress at the expense of others. Do this and your soul suffers. You can say that there is only so much of everything in the world and that those that take must do so at the expense of others, and this is so. But you also know that people are different, they do not need the same things, as long as they have what they want they are happy. Many people would rather stay at home than go out every night, for a start. It is the same with having fun, enjoying yourself, this is what god wants for you and that is why there is so much happiness over here. But it is true happiness and not achieved at the expense of others. So get on and be happy but do not make others suffer in the doing of it.

You will have heard, from your teachers, that a lot of time is spent over here singing and playing the harp. This must be true because so many arrive over here expectng to do so. Do you play the harp and, above all, do you wish to? If the answer is 'yes' then arrangements will be made so that you may. If not, then rest assured you will not be asked to do so. Are you lucky enough to be able to sing? If you can there are choirs here who will be pleased to have you and, if your voice can be trained, and this is what you want, then that will be arranged. But, if like so many, you arrive here without the talent for either, then you are not going to be talked into it. Just think of the noise if everyone did. Even on the Earth Plane there are laws about this. So you see, from what I have told you so far, death is not the enemy you have been led to believe but, indeed, a very real friend.

I would like you to remember that, when next a person you know or love, passes it is just a parting for a time only. If you want to see them again you will. We all know that the moment of parting can be sad even if it is only for a little while. Some people feel this more than others but you should make haste to get over it and then look forward with happiness to the next meeting. In this way, you will help the departed one. Grief is a very powerful force, and can make life very difficult here for the newcomer and those trying to help it to settle. Fortunately real grief is not always felt. Much of it is self pity which may look like grief but is not the same thing and therefore does not have the same effect on the departed one. When I was cremated the church was full and frankly I was very pleased, even flattered, that so many people should take the trouble 'to pay their last respects' to a chap like me. When I was drawn to the Service by sheer force of the thought that was being sent out to me I knew who was really sorry they would not be seeing me again for a while, but there was very little real grief. All the Spiritualists present knew they would see me again. I can tell you, however, if the church had been full of grief I would have been given a bad time, for its vibrations are so strong.

At this point I can tell you that cremation is the best way to dispose of the body. Some people think it is wrong, it is not. The Earth is for the people living there and not to be cluttered up with graves. The soul is very happy in the spirit world and does not like to be thought of as ing 'up in the Cemetery'. Then there is the question of keeping the grave tidy and flowers, which are expensive these days, have to be seen to be there. All this is pointless. The departed one is alive, happy and well and that is how they wish to be thought of. The best way to remember them is not at the grave side but at home, when you can sit down quietly and think about them and talk to them, by thought or out loud. Make it a certain time of the day that suits you. In the evening for example when work is finished for the day, just talk to them and they will be with you. They will also help, if they can, but do not be sad, be happy, for it will help them and you. Anyway, after all I have told you you should be happy. The last point on cremation. Some people think that it causes the departed soul pain or discomfort but this is not so. A very short time, after passing, the soul is free of the body altogether.

Chapter 4

After you have had your time of rest, you are free to settle down to your life in the Spirit World, which has become as solid to you as the Earth Plane was when you were there. Everything, the ground you stand on, the houses you live in, the birds, the trees, the animals and flowers all are solid to you. This I can well believe is quite a surprise to you but it is so and you will have to accept it! You are now living in a real world, not sitting on clouds or anything like that, so off we go to live in this real world. First there is the question of accommodation. There are plenty of places to live in because people are always on the move, for one reason or another, so there is no shortage, as on Earth. I went to stay with my Sister but only because I wanted to and for no other reason. My Sister has a place quite near my Mother so I was able to visit her as well. I know you are going to say what a strange bloke we have here who would rather stay with his Sister than his Mother. The truth is that I was so much closer to my Sister when I was on Earth, and that is how it works out. Love is the one and only force that makes everthing go. Depending on the degree of Love, as it were, so you get your priorities. Well, my sister came first. Odd it may seem to you but everyone here understands it, and it works very well. Do you see how this can happen? Remember the free will that exists here. It all ties in together. You think there is a lot to learn? You are right.

The way you carry on on the Earth Plane cannot work here. So again, like a baby you are looked after until you are ready to stand on your own feet. How do people manage who have been married and perhaps more than once. Jesus was asked the same question when they sought to trick him and he said, in effect, there is no such thing as marriage here and naturally he was quite right. There is no sex here, and children are not born, so the marriage state as you understand it cannot exist. If people marry and do not have real love between them, only sex attraction, then that counts for nothing here. People could marry half a dozen times but without true love they would not be held together, and that, I am afraid, goes for the family as well. If the family is a loving one, then

17

they will all finish up together one day, but if, as happens, there is nothing between Mothers, Fathers and children then here, as on the Earth Plane, they go their own ways. If they do not want to see each other they will not. Not even at Christmas! So I went to stay with my sister and we called on my Mother and we got up to date with each other's news. My Mother has developed quite a life of her own. She was always interested in writing, as also my Sister, and she has produced some very fine short stories for children.

Does it surprise you that we write books over here? It should not. Writers from the Earth Plane go on writing if they wish, when they come here, and painters paint and where do you think all our beautiful music comes from? No, as I have said before life goes on over here in the same way but patterned on our Spirit life style. This book, for example has been written by me, over here, with assistance from my Sister and other good friends, who have been over here much longer than I have, and are well able to advise me. My thanks go to them as they do to the friend who is writing it from here through the hand of his Son who is on the Earth Plane, poor man, and is having to do all the writing there. So you see not only can we write over here but we can get the book to you, when we have the right channel to use, but more about that part of it later.

Do you ever wonder how some people can contact us and we them. It is easy when you know how but I must tell you more about the start of my life over here. In lots of ways I was lucky when I came over for I had very few habits of which to rid myself. Smoking was my only bother, and it still is. I would give anything for a cigarette but there you are. So not having too much to distract me I was able to get on with the job of finding out how to live in this wonderful new world. The first thing I was introduced to was the way of using thought to contact people over here. This must be done with care for thought is a very powerful means of communication. If you start thinking of people willy nilly, you can cause trouble, for, as with crossed lines on your telephone, you can contact two or three at once. The thing to do is to sit down, collect your thoughts and concentrate on the one you wish to contact. To start with this is not easy but, by being persistent, you master it. After that you can think of someone and be with them very quickly. Over here you can never really interrupt anyone for time means nothing. So no one is doing anything so urgent that they cannot stop and entertain you. Then again, there is nothing personal going on here, as there is on the Earth Plane. This, together with the fact that all the kind of people you are wanting to meet, are so happy and loving, that they are glad to see you anytime.

There are those poor souls who wish to hide from everyone, because of the colour of their souls but that is a different matter. Their Helpers have ways of contacting them and drawing them slowly to the Light. I cannot stress sufficiently the fact that all, no matter what they have been or done, are looked after by Helpers, and will one day take their place here with everyone else. Once they have worked hard and, I am afraid suffered, the colour of their soul will change and they will be welcomed with love, by all. Never will people point the finger, as they do on Earth. There is no need, the colour does not become acceptable until all spirit sin has been removed. On Earth, once a person has been to prison for his crime society does not want to forget it. He has paid, yes, but he is branded. Over here we all know that God loves us and wants us all to be happy together. If He can forgive, then so do we. It could be the same on the Earth Plane, if only you would understand God's love for you all.

Punishment must be handed out, but the punishment of the soul is carried out to correct it and this is done with love and understanding and not out of revenge. The crimes the soul is punished for are those carried out on the Earth Plane when still in the body; not petty crimes, but crimes against other souls such as pushing drugs for personal gain. Using girls and children for profit. You know the kind of thing I mean. On Earth you have laws and without them you could not keep order, but many crimes do not matter too much. It is crime against the soul that is really going to have to be paid for. But we think the wonderful message is that there is no sin which will stop God loving us and if we truly repent, then we are forgiven and the work starts putting the colour right and that is the punishment. I really hope that I have made myself clear, for the teaching on the Earth Plane is different. You cannot confess your sins to man. You can, but it will not do your soul any good at all and in the same way no man can forgive you. It is just not the way of things. People are led to believe that giving money to the church will buy them favours in this world. Not at all. If you give money with love in your heart because the church needs it, then there is some merit in that, as with all giving in that manner, but please do not think that money buys anything in this life. I have said enough on this subject. The next thing is how time is spent over here, and that brings us to our next chapter.

Chapter 5

Let me say at once that, over here, there is no night or day so when I say 'day by day' it is just an expression that you will understand, that is all. How do I explain this timelessness? It is hard, for night and day are such an important part of your life cycle. You need your sleep you say. In fact it is your body that does, the soul does not and therein lies the difference. In this life you do not become tired and need to rest. On the Earth Plane, if you were kept without sleep the body would not be able to carry on, over here, the earth body has gone and so has the need for sleep. At the beginning it is rather strange to go without sleep and if you remember what I said about the habits you bring over with you, you will understand that sleep is one of them so, to start with you take your rest in the same way as you did on Earth. This habit goes, however, with time and together with all the other habits you cannot indulge in fades away to nothing.

Let me repeat once more about the habits you bring over with you for they are just as real here to start with, as they are on the Earth Plane, and you know if you have tried to give things up, how painful this can be. Drugs and smoking are the ones that give most trouble for they make such an impression on the soul. Why this should be I cannot tell you for sure. Some say it is because of the enjoyment they give at the time, an enjoyment which with most people goes on throughout their waking day. If you think about it there is something in this. People who like their food and drink tend to overdo it at certain times of the day or night although except for the unfortunates who really drink all day, most do not. Smokers on the other hand will reach for a cigarette as soon as they come to in the morning and smoke more or less non stop for the rest of the day. Be this as it may, my earnest advice to you is to come over here with as few 'hang ups' as possible. People may think that, as they become older, a lot of their habits go. This is not necessarily so. Perhaps the need for food will become less and also sex. But smoking and drinking can certainly go on with age.

It is one thing to try giving up smoking and drinking on the Earth Plane, when you know that if you are not up to the effort, you can start again. Over here you cannot do this. Your habit of almost a lifetime comes to a sudden stop with your passing, and so if, by driving home this point, I can save you the agony I know you are going to suffer, then I will have done some good for both of us. The reason for writing this book is to make you start to think about this life to which you will surely come. And your call does not always come with old age, you know that, so try and have your habits under control for you never know when the call will come. Instead of thinking, I must make the most of this life, which only lasts a short time by your standards, you should in your own best interest be thinking of this next life which I can assure you is so wonderful. Do not spoil your entry over here by having all these habits which will spoil the quality of Life. Now, have I said enough to help you, to make you think? Do not be afraid, you will have lots of loving help and understanding but you must realise that in the end, it is you who will suffer, as always.

So, let us pass on. The day, for you, has started in the World of Spirit. You have had some rest for you are still under the influence of your Earth life. You do not know what you are going to do. Remember there are no chores to attend to, as on the Earth Plane, none. No bed to make, no washing, no cleaning of teeth, no breakfast and no cigarette. Newspapers yes and books, these you have, but, of the Earth Plane nothing else. So what do you do? You can go out onto the verandah of your house and breathe in the wonderful air. There is nothing here to pollute it, no smoke, no motor cars or anything likely to spoil things. The air is perfect and it seems to sparkle. We do not need to breathe this air, as you do on Earth, but it is there, nevertheless, for our well being. It gives the soul the energy it needs. Then you look out over the beautiful landscape and, when I say that, I do it no justice at all. On the Earth Plane you have some wonderful beauty spots, as I know well, but here it is quite different. Your house is not one of a row or a block of flats, and they have not been built close together to save land or because of services, such as water, gas and so on. Also there are no factories or coal pits which need workers and therefore housing for them. No, each house is built to give pleasure to the soul living in it, and so they are all arranged to take advantage of the magnificent view. There are hills and dales, there are streams, lakes and rivers and yes, we have the sea. We must, otherwise what would become of the fish and all the other marine life. They are all here, all of them. Then there are the flowers and the trees and everywhere the wonderful green grass. How can I do justice to all this? I only hope that you will imagine all the beautiful places you have seen and then give them this special sparkle that we have here, and the colour that never fades, and the birds. How happy they are and how they let you know it. All the trees and the grass have such a beautiful shade to them. It is alive.

The water also. It sparkles. Water plays a very big part in our life over here. Not to drink, not to wash in, but to bathe in. Especially when we first arrive it is used to refresh the soul and bring it back to spirit life, after all that time on Earth. We bathe in it just as you do, except the temperature is always right. We have beautiful waterfalls as well, and the gardens to the houses have fountains. So much water, so much beauty. I can tell you, having been blind for years, to find myself looking at all this was nearly too much for me. I did not know what to think or say. Fortunately, my Sister had foreseen this and was able to help me. You really do need the help you are given when you first arrive, in every way, but that is something that should give you joy. The knowledge that when you pass over you meet with those who love you and do everything to help you settle down. You notice I do not say 'will try and help you' no, they know exactly how to help you, and they do it with love. I cannot stress this enough. You need have no fear of passing. It is a time of great joy. Please believe this. It is terrible the way people on the Earth Plane look upon death. They say 'poor old so and so has just died, did not live long enough to enjoy his retirement' and so on. How wrong they are! Old so and so is having a jolly good retirement thank you. The best.

Now the time has come to go out and meet one's friends. They are contacted by thought, no telephone here. So one sits down and thinks hard about the person one wishes to meet. This sets up a wave, and the wave finds the person. It gives him a buzz, as it were, so that he or she knows you are on the way. At the same time this wave directs you to the place the person in question is at that time. Off you go, and as you are expected, all is ready for your visit. Other people may contact you in the same way if they wish to see you. So there is no waste of time. Everything happens at quite a speed. Your journey may be long from a distance point of view but the ground is covered very quickly. If it is a meeting you are attending, then you are taken there by thought wave, and the other people will have been called by the same thought wave also. We do have meetings, quite big ones in fact. These are for special reasons such as mass healing of the very sick. At times like this we are all called to give concentrated power to the person given the healing. The healing is of the soul, not the kind of healing we can give you on the Earth Plane. The sick ones are lying on couches in the centre of the Arena. There are tier upon tier of seats all round. To say it is a little like the Albert Hall in London, is only to point your thoughts in the right direction. It is a very beautiful place, not dark as the Albert Hall, but filled with a pale, pale blue pinky light and, in the background, the soft music that we have everywhere here. At such a meeting the sick are those who are too ill to be helped by normal helpers. I have already mentioned how some teaching on the Earth Plane has such an effect on a soul that, when they arrive here they cannot accept the reality of what has happened to them and remain in the religious straight jacket that their Earth teaching has formed about their souls. This condition needs very strong power to break it and that is why we are all here, to produce that power.

First the music gives the waves upon which this power will form. then the singing from all those present adds to this. That, and the loving thoughts that are sent out, all build up, until the power is strong enough to do the job required. We can see this power building up and it is quite beautiful. It is in the form of what I can only describe as a cloud. It goes on forming with the singing and the loving thoughts until the dome of the hall we are in is filled with it. When the time is right the Master Healer calls upon the Great White Spirit, as we call god here, to send His blessing upon our meeting. So that the sick may be cured. This He does first in the form of a Dove that flies around the arena and then as a shaft of light, which falls upon the Healer himself. As this happens, all the power that has formed comes down the shaft of light like a ball of light, and rests on the head of this wonderful person. Then, armed with this power he sets about healing those souls one by one. As we watch it seems, indeed, as if each has been bound with invisible rope, for as the Healer comes to them, they struggle as if they are bound and that one by one the strands are being broken. When at last they struggle no more, the Healer takes them by the hand and lifts them to their feet. Whereupon the helpers come forward and lead them away to rest. It is wonderful to take part in such meetings and frankly I cannot do the occasion justice in these words. To explain the wonderful atmosphere created by so much love by so many people, the singing and the music.

23

Then the Dove and the divine light. Dear reader, it is too much to ask but do try and do the best you can with what I am able to give. One day you will see it for yourself and you will say 'so that is what he was trying to tell me'.

Now we must move onto other things. You will remember I told you that we had many friends over here, more than we think, and they are all delighted to see you again and you them. Arrangements have to be made, therefore, for this to happen. Thoughts are sent out and all those dear souls arrive to greet you. What a happy time it is. They remind you of this time and that and things that were important to them but which you may have forgotten. The particular thing about this meeting is that you discover how close you are to these people spiritually. You know on the Earth Plane how, at times, you meet someone and you like them at once. You do not know why but they seem your kind of person. So they are, and more than you think, for they have a spirit link with you which will ensure that you go through life together, not on the Earth Plane but in the Spirit World. They and some who are still on the Earth Plane will form the group that you will work in. It is a wonderful feeling to find out about this for at last you feel secure.

You will have to admit, from your experience on the Earth Plane to date, that you have felt let down from time to time. You are knocking along nicely and you think everything is fine when it happens and then you think you are never going to trust anything or anyone again. Very few people escape this and the net result is that we finish up feeling insecure although you would not admit it for the world. But when you find yourself in your group you feel a great sense of relief, you really are home at last. I have now experienced this and so I can talk about it. You will find that you have not met all your soulmates, as we will call them, and the chances are you may not, only a few. This is the first surprise and a very pleasant one it is too. Just think of walking into a crowded room and knowing that each and everyone there loves you and wishes you well, and that will be for the rest of your long, long wonderful life over here. With this kind of knowledge, how can you be anything else but happy? Not at once, I grant you, for it is just too much to take in at first, but come to accept it you do, and when at last you are able to accept your new situation, it is the most wonderful feeling in the world. You are, from now on, working for the good of the group. You may all be doing different things but the self element has gone. You meet and

24

discuss your work or you ask advice, anything, but always with the knowledge that all are interested and each and everyone will help the other, always. Then there is the question of helping the soulmates who are still on the Earth Plane. There are many ways we can do this but again, more about that later.

For the time being then let us talk about the group over here. They are not isolated bodies in competition with others. The group is like a spirit family to which you belong. Over here we all mix freely in the area we find ourselves in, for want of a better way of putting it. At the beginning of this book I told you, you finish up in the area that suits you best when you arrive over here. It is forever the same and you will never be able to live in an area that does not suit you. On the Earth Plane you can. It does not matter how you make your money, you can live where you like if you can afford it and there is nothing to stop you. It does not matter what you are like as a person, the money does the trick. Over here the thing that decides is the colour of your soul. That is the real you, and I am sure you can understand that very well. There you are then. You now know that, in fact, you are part of a group, and that they are all busy trying to help you through your Earth Life. The next time a piece of advice comes into your mind it could very well be your group at work and that goes for some of the strange things that happen and that turn out to be to your benefit. You are not alone ever, even if it does seem like it at times. Ask for help. All your soulmates are doing God's bidding. Now I have told you that, you must never be afraid or lonely ever again. We know it is hard for you to take this in. On the other hand we know you feel you wish it were so. So you see the seed of knowledge is already there in your soul.

The hardest thing for you to understand, at the moment, is that the Earth body is not the real you though, for as long as you can remember, you have always had it in one form or another. But the truth is the body is only a vehicle for the soul, during the time you are on Earth. Some call the body clothing for the soul. O.K. call it that, but do not call it the real you. Once you have come to terms with this fact you will start to realise that becoming old is not such a bad thing, you have gone through life, in a certain manner, and your soul has picked up good marks and bad on the way. If it had not the chances are you would not be normal. Looking back you can see the mistakes you have made and you will perhaps also see that, at the time, you had a choice. You choose a certain path and certain results followed. You always have a choice and that is the only way the soul may learn and gain experience, can you see that? If you are always being put on the right path then you would cease to be you. You would just be carrying out someone elses wishes. You should not be too worried about the trouble you get into because you chose to take the path you did. Most of the trouble is physical or of the body not of the soul. It is damage caused to the soul that must be paid for before it can be put right. You can say that the damage done to other people's souls is worse still, and must be paid for more heavily. So where does this little homily leave you? Worried? Do not be, for it is possible that if you are reading this you have nothing to fear.

We are not given a very clear lead, on the Earth Plane, as to the true meaning of sin. Most of the teaching is about mortal sin and up to a point this is right for you must learn discipline on the Earth Plane in order to lead an orderly life there. Also, it is the soul's place of learning, and the soul must learn discipline. This is most important for as I have said before, there is free will over here and nothing to stop the soul from doing what it likes, once it is free of the body. If the soul has learned its lesson, had its good times and its bad, then it arrives here with a good grounding and is then able to carry on with its higher education. That is why it is better for the soul if it has taken a bit of a buffeting on the Earth Plane, rather than a protected, trouble-free life. You may say, but I thought you said my group are there to help me, they are, just as people try and help their children with their homework. But the homework must be done, one way or another. What your helpers do is to try and stop you having trouble that will do no one any good. The fact that they do not always succeed cannot be held against them. There are sometimes forces on the Earth Plane that are much stronger and it is at this point that we find ourselves coming to the question of evil. Evil you have heard about, seen or suffered from. It is around and in quite large quantities. Everything is not gladness and light as we would wish it to be. Evil is a condition of mind. As you have those who are good, you have others who are bad. You could say that there is a little evil in all of us, to start with, but when the time comes to choose we choose to be good. The choice again.

Chapter 6

The choice is ours. We are given the best advice but it is always left to us to decide which course we will take. This was so on Earth and it is the same over here. As I have said this must always be as otherwise we would not be ourselves. There is a lot more to be taken into consideration over here, however, for you have the group to consider. You are very much a part of it now, so your choice is discussed if you and the group are to benefit and not just you. In fact the group does benefit from what experience you have encountered. Now the choice you make cannot be anything other than good, at this stage, for by now the soul has passed the point where evil can take a hand. So you get down to choosing how you are going to pass your time here to start with. In my case I wanted very much to write this book. As it happened my group had not had a writer on their hands before, so they were only too pleased to have me do this. Not only that but they would also like to take a hand in it. So you see, when I proudly write that this is written by Ken Akehurst, I should also say 'And Group'. But then we are going to have enough trouble getting people on the Earth Plane to believe that this is written from Spirit, as it is, without that.

We are, in fact, going to have a success with this book. I can tell you this, for we can see far enough into the future to make this statement. This fact fills us with joy. Not because we are vain but because the people who will read it will be helped, by us, and that is what our life is all about now. If over a million read it, and well they might, just think of that. They may not all be helped, but most will, and so we cannot help being filled with joy. Would you pass up a chance to help so many at one go?

The reason it will be such a success is that it is all true, one hundred per cent true. Not written for effect, as some are, by people on the Earth Plane who do it for this and for money. Their efforts are of no value, whatsoever, in the spirit sense. They are just writing for gain. We have set out to keep everything we say easy to read. Easy to understand and therefore as easy to believe, as possible. We know we shall have many

27

critics and we welcome this, for if they can express doubts we can provide reason in our answers. In this way we will be able to help even more people. Having found this channel, through which to reach the Earth Plane it would not be very bright, on our part, not to use it to the full. This piece of information may not fill the poor chap who must do all the writing on the Earth Plane with joy, but there it is. He said he would do it so he is stuck with us. We know in his heart he enjoys it so we do not mind too much but we can promise you you will be hearing a lot more from us after this book. We have got the bit between our teeth and also having gained this experience, we feel that it would be a great waste to make this writing a one-off job.

We may as well, while we are on the subject, tell you how all this came about. You must be interested. Well, the person over here who is doing the actual writing, was very close to his son on the Earth Plane and, because of this, stayed close to him after he passed on. Not because he could not accept the fact that he had passed on, but because his choice of work was to help his son through the bad time he could see was ahead of him on the Earth Plane. Having set out to do this, and we are happy to say he has succeeded, he found that he was able to impress thoughts into the mind of this lad. After that it was not long before he found he could use spirit power to move his hand. Then came the task of learning how to write all over again. This took quite a time, but by long hours of practice he became good enough for us to start. I knew his son, for a little while, on the Earth Plane before I came over here so you see everything fitted in very well. All this was not luck or coincidence. It had been worked upon for a long time by people over here. That is more or less how the writing came about but the question of choice was always there. Anywhere along this path, a choice could have been made to make this work impossible. So you see choice is a very important thing and if the wrong one is made it can have unfortunate effects. So the book was written by me, with the aid of my group and now it is being copied by our two friends, father and son. By the way we are told that about a thousand hours over nine months was the time taken in practicing the writing. Quite a time and a lot of paper and ink!

Now let us get on with our message to you and those you are good enough to pass this book onto. The choice, which becomes so important to us all the more we think of it, really is how one's life unfolds. How we make our choice, which is ours alone, decides our life and at the same time tells us and all interested parties, what we are like

28

as people. First on Earth and then in Spirit, for, whatever we get up to is recorded by the soul. This in turn, decides the colour of the soul which then decides how things will work out for you when you arrive over here. What is it that decides the choice we make? A good question! We have lots of good advice from friends but there are still times when we delight in putting our foot in it. Why should this be? We have talked and talked about this and we think it must be a deep-seated longing, by the soul, for experience, even if it is not going to turn out to be pleasant in the end. If you think of this it could be the answer. If you go through life and do not put a foot wrong how are you going to understand and help those who do? If you have always made the right choice you are going to finish up in a class on your own and will find it hard to mix with others. Allright you say, but what about the soul that passes over very young, the baby and the child. There are plenty of them over here, what chance have they to start making choices? Well they do when they are old enough but instead of having the Earth as a school they have the World of Spirit. These choices, being purely of the spirit, prepares them for a much higher life. This is a fact of spirit life and we cannot tell you any more about it. All we know is that we are all very happy for them. And that is about all we can usefully say about choice, but remember much of what we say is just to get you thinking. If you make what seems to be a bad choice, it may well finish up being good for you in some way in the end.

Chapter 7

You may find this hard to believe but we do have field work to do. It is not quite what you think, however, but is rather like the work missionaries do on the Earth Plane. We work with souls who, for one reason or another, will not come to terms with the fact that their life on Earth is over. Because their idea of 'death' does not add up to the state they find themselves in, they tend to think that they are still on the Earth Plane. This as you can guess gives them problems, which are not easy to overcome. The first snag is our old friend free will. As long as they continue to think they are still alive and on the Earth Plane they are. The next snag is the time factor. As there is no such thing as time they are always in a 'now' situation, and this goes on and on. The fact that their loved ones on the Earth Plane do not say anything to them or take any notice does not always strike them as being strange either. We have a lot of difficulty with these people because all the help they need can only come when they accept their new condition. It is very rewarding work for us for it is the basic kind of help the soul needs, so our success is all the more important. When we are able to get such a one to accept his new position or condition, it is a great joy to all, for there is nothing so terrible as seeing a soul in this state, in limbo, so to speak, not in your world or this, with all the frustrations of trying to make themselves heard or trying to make sense of what is going on. It is hell for them, and real suffering.

How do we set about helping such a one? Well if we are lucky enough to know someone who knows them, someone who has passed over and is known to the soul in question, then we get them to have a word with them. The snag is that most of those who find themselves in this state have come over as a result of an accident, a national disaster or something like that, and have therefore bypassed the normal way of dying and being taken care of. People who take their own lives are in this condition but as they have committed a sin against the soul we are not in a position to help them. How do we know the difference? By the colour of their souls. They are not left without hope, it is just that they are a different class of soul and must be treated by special helpers who are trained to handle such people. People should know that to take ones own life is the most damaging thing of all. You may think this is hard but it is the choice the soul has and it is the wrong one. The right one is to stay and live out the problems life has set you.

Most things are in the mind. How many times have things turned out not to be as bad as you thought. Plenty I'll bet. The big trouble is that whatever caused the suicide comes over with the soul and causes as much agony as it suffered in the first place. This is part of the punishment. Not a nice subject, is it, but it must be spoken of so as to try to stop people doing it. They should be given help on the Earth Plane. There should be more places and people for this kind of soul to turn to for help. They do not do this kind of thing on the spur of the moment. It is a condition of mind, that is building up over a period of time and in most cases there is always someone who knows that this terrible act is on the cards and could prevent it if they took the trouble. You see, really, there is first of all a cry for help before the final step is taken, and it is a wicked thing not to do so in a case like this. I know you can think up all sorts of things to prove me wrong but at the end of the day you will know I am right. There is always the cry for help and, if that is not forthcoming, the final step is taken.

Now let us get on with this life over here. We have talked about quite a few aspects of it but there is so much else to tell you, things, we hope, that will make your heart glad. Do you remember, I told you that we have rivers to swim in, also lakes and streams, and they provide us with much pleasure and are very good for the health of the soul. When our labours are done for the day we take ourselves off for a swim. Not as you do, let me hasten to add. We do not need swim suits or towels, we just go in as we are. The water is perfectly real to us but it is not like your water, in as much that we do not get wet and therefore do not need to change. Very strange you may think. Well yes, but not to us. We dive in and swim about and of course we can float. The thing is we can all do this and we do not have to learn to do it. Those among us who were good at swimming on the Earth Plane are even better over here, and they have races and games just as when they were on the Earth Plane.

This brings me to the question of sport over here. The short answer is that we have everything you enjoy on Earth. Strange? Why should it be? Sport is able to give so much pleasure to so many people, and that

31

kind of enjoyment must be encouraged. Besides, what would all our sportsmen do when they come over here? We are all of us as keen to watch them play as we ever were and they are only too keen to go on doing that which they can do best. Games of every kind are arranged here, in the same way as on Earth. Football is just as popular and is organised in the same way, so is cricket. As on Earth each game has its following, the only thing is we do not have seasons, so games go on all the time. How do you manage about time, if you have no clocks to play by? Well, we have a system to take care of that. We know when changes should be made, just as we know when it is time to stop working, or anything else we are doing. You cannot really think that the absence of a clock can bring all our sporting activities to a halt can you! We know all about the big money there is in sport on the Earth Plane these days and have our own thoughts about it. Let me just say that we do literally thank God that we do not have that problem here and that goes for the crowd. They enjoy themselves but there is not the violence you have. It may surprise you to know that quite a few souls make the journey back to Earth to watch some of your games. It is not quite the same for them as it is for you. The light on Earth is not very good to spirit eyes, but it is good enough and worth the effort for those keen enough to do it.

So you can see, as my story unfolds, life goes on over here in many ways as before but the quality is very much improved. Can you imagine what sport here is like when it is played for the love of it? Just pure skill coming to the fore with no bad tempers or fouls to spoil it. If you are a sports lover you now have something else to look forward to when you come over. I have not mentioned tennis but that is very popular here, just as it is with you, also there is horse racing. I will not go on but just say 'everything you have we have, but better!' By taking the mystery and the fear out of death, and putting, in its place, the certain knowledge of the truth and the joy of this life, gives me much joy.

Chapter 8

Ever since I came over here, I have wanted to tell the people of the Earth Plane what a beautiful place the Spirit World is, but I have not managed to do this very well so far. So now I am going to have a real try. Although you do have many beauty spots on Earth they do not have anything like the quality and the beauty of those over here and because of this I cannot use any of them as examples. Beauty is what you seek on the Earth Plane and since the car has become within the reach of most people, you are making for it in large numbers. We can understand this for much of the surroundings where people live are rather grim and your places of work can be even worse. So it is natural that you should wish to get away to the sea or the countryside, for what you see as beauty and fresh air. Somewhere or other you will finish up in a traffic jam and, to us, an awful time of sitting in heat and fumes. You seem to mind this, but not that much, for you forget all about it and gladly set off to do it again the next chance you get. Well the first piece of good news is that we do not have the car over here. When we wish to go somewhere we have the means of doing so, ourselves, and it is without effort. We can quickly cover big distances either with friends or on our own. Wherever we go here, it is beautiful.

The countryside has been developing for countless years. Some parts are natural landscape, others have been developed by landscape spirits who carry on their work here when they arrive. Those who have worked on the land or in gardens on the Earth Plane have a real love for it, going on with their work for their pleasure and our delight. As this has been the way of things for countless years you can believe some very wonderful things have been achieved. I know on your television sets you are shown lovely gardens and parks and they do your heart good. Well, just try and picture what it must be like here, after all those clever people have been able to use their talents but with flowers and shrubs of such colour and beauty they cannot be described. It is breath taking and there is so much of it, for they are not limited for space. They do not have to worry about roads or factories or private land. They can go on developing their skills and the land to their heart's content. Now do not think these green-fingered people go around doing this on their own. Not at all. As with most things, over here, it is a group effort and each and every project is thought about and talked about until the best possible plan is produced. so you see, as we go along our way we come across some landscaping or a flower garden that has been planned and arranged exactly to suit that particular spot or area. Always there are benches or grassy banks to rest upon. Then you may come upon a glade of trees. I could have said leafy but really they are not, for we do not have seasons and leaves do not fall as they do on Earth. But the grass always grows however many trees there are and there is always a pale light no matter how thick the leaves. And as I have said, rivers, lakes and streams everywhere. Pools and waterfalls, brooks and lily ponds with fish and frogs, dragonflies, birds, everything. But no bites nor stings, just the beauty of them all.

So that I could write something worthwhile for you, I went on a journey and took a few notes of what I saw and the people I met on the way. So here we go. I left my sister's house with her for company. It was, as always, a beautiful day as we set off for the distant hills. The grass underfoot was springy and easy to walk on. (It is the first time I have set off on a journey like this since my arrival.) We made for the hills, to begin with so that I could be given a good view of the area we were living in. As we made our ascent we passed clumps of bushes and then trees until we were at last clear of them and had nothing to interrupt our view. For me this was truly a wonderful experience because for years I had been unable to walk too far owing to diabetes which left me feeling very tired. Then, in the latter years, I lost my sight, so you see to be able to walk up hill without effort and to be able to see where I was going was quite something and I made the most of it. When we had gone far enough to obtain the view we wanted we stopped and my sister pointed out her house and that of my mother. From this height they looked like doll's houses and just as pretty. All the houses, (quite a few are bungalows), were situated at the foot of the hill opposite, and a little way up. They were not in rows but dotted about and facing in different directions, each surrounded by trees and hedges with lots of colourful flower beds surrounding the houses themselves. All this made a very brave show indeed and gave one some idea as to the love and care that had gone into the planning of the whole area.

34

I would like to tell you that we sat down and had a picnic but I am afraid we did not. What we did was to go on climbing to the top of the hill so that we could appreciate the view on the other side. It is always a wonderful feeling to stand at the top of a high hill and be able to look around you and at the view below. But this had an added beauty for me. Never have I known the air to sparkle so much. Never had I seen a sky like this, pale azure tinted with the palest of pink and without a hint of a cloud. Not much good for harping here, you will see! Then when we looked down into the valley below we could see a river winding away into the distance like a silver ribbon sparkling between its deep green banks. Over here it seems that you can see much further than on Earth. Anyway, a long, long way off we could see a ridge of mountains that had many shades of green upon them and at the foot a lake into which the river seemed to flow. One really does get a feeling of space over here, never the feeling of crowding one gets on Earth. so far we have not met a soul.

Having taken in the beauty of that valley and the mountains in the distance, we continued our walk along the ridge which formed the top of our hill, down into the saddle and then along a ridge which ran lower down from the top until we came to quite a large hollow with trees and bushes growing in it and, at the far end, a house just visible in the trees, which seemed to be built of marble for it gleamed white against such a dark background. I asked my Sister who lived there and she told me to wait and see for we were going to call there. And so we did. As we walked up the long winding approach to the house through a long line of trees that made a tunnel with their overhanging branches and leaves we could hear children singing. When we arrived at the house we could see that it was indeed a large one with wide shallow steps leading up to a verandah that ran the whole length of the house, more or less, with a fine large open doorway in the centre. There were doorways leading off the verandah along both sides of the main doorway and at each end there were doorways facing inwards. There were no curtains, as such, but a muslin type of material that I have already mentioned before.

The singing had stopped by the time we had reached the verandah but children's voices could be heard. We walked into the main hallway and to our left and there was an office with 'Headmaster' printed on a sign situated half-way up what would have been the door had there been one, but in its absence, was fixed to the wall. Sitting behind a desk was a rather thick-set looking man. Not old and not young either.

On seeing my Sister and me standing there he rose from behind his desk and with a big smile and arms outstretched he bade us enter. I was just about to meet the first headmaster, of a child's school, in a very long time. To keep the story short this man and my sister were old friends and he also knew my Mother well so I was another one of our family for him to get to know. Hence the visit. It was also a chance for me to widen my knowledge of the life over here.

You will remember I spoke about the children over here before, and how happy they were. Now I was to see them at their studies. We were taken along from class to class so that I could see for myself how lessons were conducted. Much to my surprise each classroom, which opened onto the verandah, was very much the same as the classrooms well known to children on the Earth Plane. A blackboard ran along one wall, in front of which was a low platform with a desk and chair for the teacher. The children sat at desks facing. The number of children per class would be between ten and twelve, but the most striking thing was that they were of different nationalities. The white children and the coloured all happily learning together. In this day and age there is nothing very odd in this. Most schools could show you the same on the Earth Plane. No, the thing was that there were coloured children. I suppose for some reason that is not very clear to me now, I always thought the soul was white. That the colour was of the body only and that was all. How wrong could I be! The Headmaster explained, for the sake of my simple mind, that children from all over the world were passing over all the time. That like grown-ups they kept their own identity and it would be very odd indeed if suddenly this system changed. When you think of it this is how it must be. You become younger in appearance but other than that you look, in spirit, very much as you did on the Earth Plane, so how can you change your colour, and anyway it would be an insult if you did, and that could never happen here.

Well, here I am learning all the time. What kind of subjects are they taught? I can hear you ask. Very much the same as on the Earth Plane but as it applies to the spirit world. They must learn to read and write. They need maths, history, geography and as they become older they have more advanced subjects. Then they have music lessons, art and so on. They have singing lessons, they have games and go swimming. In fact normal things for normal children. The headmaster assured me that they were not little angels, and that some were brighter than others, but, as time was of no moment, time could be spent with the slow ones without holding back the brighter.

Here the question of language has been brought up. How is it that with so many different tongues being spoken on the Earth Plane we can all understand each other over here. The short answer is we cannot. We are all just the same as on the Earth Plane, from that point of view. This also goes for the area we live in, East is East and West is West and that is how it must remain. With free will the soul is free to travel if it wishes and if learning another language is what you wish to do, then so you shall. All things are possible over here. But now let me get back to my story. The children although of different nationalities are English speaking. Their parents were living in Great Britain when they were born, so it is natural that they should wish to stay in this area. If they had wanted to go to another area for family reasons, then that is what they would have done. Even at a very tender age the soul has a will of its own. Not only do the children attend school here in this large white house, they also live here, they have rest rooms and play rooms on the first floor. Their teachers also live here, in fact just as everything is arranged on the Earth Plane. Also, they will stay here until their development is such that they must move on.

It is all very natural and no pressure is put upon them at all. That is why they are so happy here, they are allowed to live as children. Nothing else is expected of them. No parental pride pushing them on. No competition with other children enters their lives. They are left to develop naturally. This does not mean that they are not taught to behave or understand discipline. They are, but it is taught as a subject, and not, as happens so often on the Earth Plane, slapped into them. All in all, these children are having a marvellous life over here. So if you know of someone who has 'lost' a child, as you put it, then please give them this good news. The teachers are such wonderful people, who love the job they are doing and the children, so you see the parents can be assured that their little loved one is happy and being well looked after. We can understand them being missed, but do not be sad for them. Also you should know they have visits from such relations as are over here, so the family link is kept up, and the parents will see them again when the time is right. No one will forget.

In many parts of the world at Christmas time, the spirit children are remembered. Sometimes gifts are brought and dedicated to them, before they are given to children on the Earth Plane. I want to tell you that this is a wonderful idea and the children here love it. They understand very well what it is all about and they enjoy the link that is formed between themselves and the children on Earth. So many children on Earth can really see our children here, and it is quite wonderful to see the joy that this brings to both. Those over here have plenty of toys of their own and cannot have the ones you dedicate to them, but this they understand and it does not concern them. It is the link that is formed at the time, that gives them so much joy. That, and the fact that the gifts give so much happiness to your children. So, for as long as you can, please keep this practice going and know that you are giving pleasure to so many.

Now the time has come to leave the school and make our way home. Did we see any rabbits or other wild life on our way to the school you may ask! Yes we did, plenty, and it was remiss of me not to mention them. All these creatures are here and, like everyone else, are enjoying their life very much. All the fear has gone out of their lives at last so they are able to play about, in the open, as they so love to do. They have a lot of fun and so do we watching them, and the children love them most of all. I have told you that you will meet your pets again when you come over and so you will. All have souls and will endure just as you and I. They will, however, always remain animals. They cannot develop in any other way, and I do not think they would have it differently. They love you just as you love them, and as always it is this bond which keeps you together. They will wait for you to arrive over here, like the rest of us, and a real old fuss there will be when you do. This idea of their souls going into a kind of pool and then back to Earth is wrong. In a sense they are people and as such go on as people. I hope I have put your mind at rest on this point. They come to Earth to see you quite often. They come with your guides and friends, in fact, sometimes there are more animals around you than people, especially if you love them. They may not all be yours but you may have made friends with them over the years. I tell you, love is the thing that decides so much in this life. In fact it needs a chapter on its own and will get it.

Well we arrived home at last. It had all been very wonderful and I was happy to sit and think about it all. The happy children, the happy teachers and then the happy wild life and not least the happy us. Why all this happiness? On Earth we have flashes of happiness and are grateful for them but there is always someone or something, at hand, to spoil it. Why then does that not happen over here? It must be the body, but this cannot be so for it is only the vehicle or clothing. If the soul is always happy over here, why not over there? It could be quite easily if you would only let it. The key word is materialism. Over here there is none. Now, you will say that you are living in a material world, and no one can argue with that, but I fear the maggot in the apple is greed. There are too many people who are greedy, and want more than their fair share. Once upon a time a few were greedy, and the rest managed with what they had. Looking back they realise that they were happy enough. Now, however, this greed has taken hold of most, and it is only the few who are not, and it is this that is causing so much unhappiness. If only people could be made to see this. If only they would realise that the greed, the grabbing, the envy and jealousy, and all the other things that go with them, and there are plenty, lead to crime and so on. All this has a shocking effect on the soul, and gives it a terrible colour. Life on Earth is only of a short duration so why use that time in grabbing things you really do not need, and certainly cannot take with you, at the expense of the soul, which you must. If only that was universally understood there would be happiness on Earth. There is plenty for all if you just take what you need and you would then arrive over here with a soul we could all be proud of. Do not doubt the truth of this. You have the chance to do this, but you choose to be selfish and grabbing, so when you arrive here things are not so good. I speak of man generally but it could also be you. If you are still young enough to change your ways, then it would be a good idea to do so. If not, well you will have the chance to put it right later.

Chapter 9

You may think that I have already covered what you can expect, in what I have told you to date. Yes, in a way, but not in much detail. I have told you what happens when dying and how you will be looked after. I have not told you what happens if you do not have a normal passing. At a time like this you are a stranger in a strange land not met by a friend or loved one. Because it happens frequently arrangements have been built up over time so that this is taken care of. There are Helpers who are trained to deal with this situation. The first thing they look for is the colour of your soul. There are Helpers for different shades and colours. In other words there are different Helpers for different grades of souls. You must not be surprised at this for you know as well as we do, that people can be classed as good, not so good and so on. You do this on Earth where even bad ones are divided into different classes. Thus depending upon the state of their souls, on passing, they need specialised care. Far better for the soul to be caught and made to understand its new status, for then the task of putting it right can begin. If it is allowed to go unhelped it is most distressing for all of us. I will tell you of one case I know of through a Helper in my group.

A young man came over here suddenly, through a car accident. His life up to date had been one of self, in every respect. He had absolutely no thought for any one but himself. The colour of his soul was ghastly for he had sunk to some pretty low tricks in his selfish life. Now the time had come to pay for this and have the matter put right. My friend the Helper was in luck at the start for the young man, being very interested in himself, wanted to know what had happened and where he was. When he was told, he could not believe it, but the truth was soon demonstrated to him. But then his bad time set in. He wanted a drink and a cigarette. He could not have them. Other things came into his mind, and the fact that someone else was going to have the money he had stolen. One way and another he became very agitated and difficult to handle. He insisted upon going back to Earth and the people he had mixed with. This did him no good at all because he saw them living the life he had been leading and no longer could and he was not too pleased about the things they had to say about him. All this added up to a lot of frustration and despair on his part and it was difficult for the Helper to persuade him to leave. When he did manage to get him away he took him home and made him welcome. Having talked to him and gained his confidence he was able to draw his life story from him. As you can imagine it did not make pleasant hearing at all and slowly this fact dawned on the young man himself. To begin with he had thought it all rather clever. Time, as you know by now, does not mean anything over here so we cannot say how long it took him to pass from being a boastful person to one filled with remorse.

But this is what happened and he then started to pay for all the wrong he had done. This is the hell people talk about and it is all self-imposed and can only happen when the soul of its own free will allows it. As long as he remained boastful he could carry on but in fact he would just be putting off the day when his treatment would start. The training the Helper is given makes it all possible. He would be an advanced soul but one that would have had trouble of its own to overcome. That is why I said, early on, how much better it is for the soul to have taken a buffeting from life rather than having had a sheltered one. Then again the Helper would give out love and understanding to this man which would eventually get through to his soul and help it to see the shoddiness of its life's quality to date. Thus by talking, by showing love and understanding the break through is made. And as medicine can break the fever and cause the healing perspiration so the evil fever in the young man was broken and his past life was seen with shame and remorse. Through all this the Helper would be with him watching the agony through which this soul would have to pass, and because there was nothing constructive the young man could do about it, it was all the more terrible. If he could have put things right with the people he had wronged it would have helped, but he could not. Well, he suffered appallingly. His Helper talked and talked with him about the things he had done until he was in a state of true repentance which only comes when the soul accepts the total degree of shame for its actions. As long as there is the slightest resistance to this state, then the suffering must continue, and you can appreciate this must be so. For the soul's own sake total repentance is the only answer. This happened and from that point on the Helper was able to return that soul to full health and colour. I have told you all this so that you may understand that sin must be paid for. It is only the free will of the soul that can allow this to happen and true repentance must be felt before God forgives you and healing takes place. The greater the sin the greater the suffering. But remember the help and the love he was given. He suffered, yes, but it was for his own good and he was never alone. Always remember God never wants you to suffer, it is your choice first and last.

There is so much to tell. As I have said earlier, although I was in the Spirit Movement on the Earth Plane I was not at all well prepared for what I found on my arrival over here. Somehow or other the true message never came across. I have sat for hours in church and at meetings and listened to mediums and their inspirers, holding forth, but never have I heard them say a word that would help a soul to prepare itself for the big change that takes place. I was told countless times, that there was no death and that I should be pleased about that. Naturally I was, and as a believer, I was happy to tell others, as best I could, so that they too could be happy. But as to what we could expect was never made very clear. Now my chance has come to try and put matters right. Please God I may make the most of it.

I have talked a little about the passing and something of what I have seen and things like that but have I, even now, given you a living picture in your mind of what it is all about? Have I really removed the mystery about the soul passing into spirit? I am not sure. Even now after all I have said if you have doubt in your mind this is going to spoil it all for you. What, I think to myself, can I say or do to make these people accept what I am saying? There seems to be, at a certain point, a mental block that will not let you realise the truth when you read it. It is very frustrating. Why, you may ask, is it so important for me to believe every word you say on this subject? Well, the first thing is we want to take the uncertainty, and therefore fear, out of the act of passing over. If you and everyone else could just understand that it is such a very natural thing to do, at a certain stage of your evolution, and that there is absolutely no mystery about it at all. You go to bed at night and generally you sleep and then in the morning you awake. Perfectly normal as far as you are concerned. The body needed its rest. Fine, well when you pass over it is as natural as that. The time has come for the soul to move on. It is not the first nor the last time the soul does this. There will be other times when the soul will move on, but only when it is ready. I must repeat this for if you come to the end of this book and are still not sold on what we have to say, we have failed. All the time and effort that has gone into the production of it wasted and, on top of that, if you will not believe what we say now, how can we tell you more in the future? No, we must make you understand, now. Which takes us on to the next chapter.

Chapter 10

When you leave the Earth Plane you do so because the time has come for you to return home. The time on Earth was a time spent away. The real you is spirit, not flesh and blood. Your body was given you as protection for your soul. You could not live without it there, whereas you could not live with it here. The fact of the matter is that you become accustomed to having a body and you cannot believe that there can be much of a life without it, whereas your life without it is immeasurably better. If you could only grasp this point, you would be well on your way to understanding a great deal of what I am telling you. The material world has been built up over countless years by man trying hard to make his stay on Earth more pleasant. The driving force was the knowledge the soul had that this life could be much better. Much has been achieved in this direction but unfortunately it has got out of hand and your material resources are beginning to run down at, what to you is an alarming rate. To you and to many this is a disaster. In fact, it is not, it could be your salvation. The world must return to a more reasonable way of life. There is no reason at all why you should be uncomfortable.

At the moment you eat too much and drink too much, as a nation, and now I speak of the United Kingdom but it is true of other nations as well. You are wasteful, food is thrown away because you have plenty of money for more. This is very wrong; food should never be wasted however much money you have. In fact as I have already said, this non-stop chasing after more and more money to buy more and more things is spoiling the quality of your life on Earth and is also doing a bad job on your soul. The reason for your being on Earth in the first place is for basic education of the soul and what do you do? Do your best to ruin it with chasing after things that really do not give you much pleasure in the end. What you should be doing is passing through this life in a happy, contented manner. Be satisfied with simple comforts. It is not necessary to buy so many of the same things. If you have a comfortable home, be satisfied, do not always be wanting to change it for new.

You may well ask what has all this got to do with me, one who is now well established in the Spirit World? The answer is, plenty. If I am to help you make the most of your education on Earth in readiness for your passing to Spirit, it is necessary to see to it that material things do not become an obsession with you. Have what you need to improve the quality of your life, yes, but do not let it get out of hand so that you must keep on having more and more, bigger and better. Someone is going to have to pay for all the unhappiness it can bring, all this fear of the future that debt can cause. Why do it? Why give yourself a bad time when all you have to do is be happy with your lot. When I was on the Earth Plane I worked all my life until blindness caught up with me. My life was not very different from lots of other chap's at that time. The money I earned bought me the things I needed, but I think the difference in those days was the fact that if you could not afford something you did not have it. That was a way of life and you were a fool and heading for trouble if you did not follow it. I think that was a very sound way of carrying on. Today everyone seems to be living above their income because the last thing they are going to do is go without anything. If they want it they borrow for it.

The fact that the cost is inflated by interest which is usually compounded does not seem to matter to start with but, when it does, the thing to do is to ask for more money from the employer, because you cannot manage on what you are receiving. This is morally wrong for, in the end, it can turn the people concerned into ugly customers. They go on strike and cause other people needless suffering and why? Because they do not have the moral discipline to buy only what they can afford and this, in turn, has a very unhappy effect on the soul which faithfully records everthing. We are able to watch all this happening and it is not a pretty sight, and we are far from happy, for we know all this must be paid for. The other people who fill us with despair are the demonstrators. Usually it seems to us they will demonstrate against anything, but if they only knew the damage they did to themselves, apart from the damage on Earth, they would not do it. If they could see the terrible clouds of hate and anger they set up they would stop. Just as clouds of love can be built up and used for healing so this evil cloud may be used by evil people. This is a very bad thing for us, over here, and naturally the souls responsible will have to pay. They will finish up paying for it and will repent, but why do it in the first place? Like so much on the Earth Plane trouble seems to be so much more attractive than good. Mankind, on a very big scale, seems to be bent on creating so much trouble for everyone and, in turn, for themselves, that it passes all understanding. It was ever so. History is full of man's inhumanity to man but must it go on? Will you never learn? Then to cap the lot there are those who blame God for it. This is too much. Man causes all the trouble and then blames God. No, you cannot get away with that any more than having caused the mess you can call on God to come in and clear it up. You cannot do that either. Some of the world's statesmen are going to have to answer for it just as many have had to do in the past. I have said enough, but if only people would think things through before they act, they would save themselves much unhappiness and certainly be in a better shape when they arrive Home.

Chapter 11

I have spoken a little about the Parting already but I have more to say for I believe there is a lot of misunderstanding on the Earth Plane about it. Again the more we talk about it the more natural and acceptable it will become. Fear of death is at the back of this, and ignorance is the cause. 'No one has ever come back to tell us' you say. Jesus did but for some reason his message is not accepted, except by a few. No, many people have 'come back' but this is only accepted by the comparative few who call themselves Spiritualists. We are pleased to say their numbers are growing all the time, but not fast enough. At the same time there are so many who still think that Spiritualism is the work of the devil. Why that should be so we are not too sure. Again, can it be because it is not understood by the majority? For myself, having seen both sides, I can see something of where the fault lies. If you believe it is possible for us, over here, to contact you, over there, then you will listen with sympathy to the messages received and given by the medium. Now sometimes the medium is not sufficiently developed and at others, the one trying to get through is not having much success. The end result is that the message is not very clear or does not make sense. If you do not know this, and if you do not know how difficult it is for Spirit to make contact anyway, then you think it is all a lot of nonsense. Also there are a few mediums who, for one reason or another, are not receiving correct advice from Spirit, and will start making up messages, and that naturally gets the movement a bad name.

But if you have a good medium and the messages really start to flow and are understood and accepted then surely there can be no better proof. There are those who go on wanting more and more proof. They can be tiresome, for they are placing the burden of proof entirely on Spirit. After the one returning has gone to so much trouble to get the message across they will be answered with a 'yes, but'. Surely you can meet Spirit half way. If you are speaking to a friend on Earth, and they are trying to explain something to you, you listen and even help them with words sometimes, but you listen and let them make their point.

Why do you change so much when a friend from Spirit tries to tell you something, and why should the devil be behind it? The messages the spirit one has gone to so much trouble to get across is always helpful, in one way or another. They first of all prove that there is no death which, heard often enough, will really sink in, and this can only be good for you. Then the message is sent with love and some helpful words for you, just as this book is. So why not say, 'Thank you dear friend for your message and all the trouble you have gone to to send it, it makes me very happy.' If you are happy they will see it and be happy themselves. Their efforts rewarded. If you do not accept it there is gloom all round. So we must continue to press upon you the fact that sooner or later you are going to make the journey home and that it is best for everyone if you arrive looking presentable so that all can be proud of you. You will if you lead a normal Christian life. By this I mean that you should follow His teaching as best you can. You will have your failures, but it is the trying that counts for it means you have accepted what He said. If you love God and your neighbour as yourself, those said Jesus are the most important commandments. You have to love your neighbour over here and you certainly love God so why not do so on the Earth Plane? We know that the word Love causes a lot of people trouble on the Earth Plane for they will equate it with physical love. And this is not what we are talking about.

We speak of Spiritual love and there cannot be anything physical about that. Jesus said Those who are not against us are for us. And that is the answer. Over here we are against no one and no one is against us. There is therefore a wonderful feeling of goodwill to all and that just about sums up our feeling of love. Please remember this book is a guide to the hereafter. It is not a religious book in the sense that you understand it. Then again, I talk as a Christian because that is what I am. We like to think that Christ's teaching is best for us to follow but this does not mean that other religions and sects are not good for their followers. They are, and they all find their way here and they are all helped and loved because God loves us all, believers and non believers alike. It is just that they have travelled a different road home. There will be the unfortunate bigots among them, as in our community, and they will be helped with love and understanding, in the same way. When all people arrive home they know the truth at last. The real and simple truth. That God loves us all and all are equal in His sight. It is the colour of your soul that counts and nothing else. All efforts are made to see

48

that all souls are returned to good health. That is what God wants and that is what we want. So with all that going for you how can you not be happy here? Death, as you call it, is not terrible, life is. Over here we do not suffer as you do. When you arrive over here you will soon see what I mean. All the aches and pains of the body go. All the other troubles of the material life go also. You are left with yourself and all the bad habits you have acquired on Earth, and all that can be a snag, as I have explained. But the atmosphere here is so wonderful. The loving thoughts that are everywhere fill you with this feeling of well being and all the tensions of the Earth Plane fall away. You will soon lose the pull of the Earth Plane but you must expect to go through it a bit if those you have left behind show real grief. It is in your best interest if they are pleased that you have passed but that is not always easy to get over to people.

The other thing they should not do is sit down and think about all the trouble there was between you and how they wish they had done things differently. This does no good at all. What was done was done and that is the end of it. All will be put right in time. The best thing you can do for the departed one, is to be genuinely happy for them that their time on Earth is over and look forward to the time when you will be with them again, for you certainly will be if that is your wish. Many people become close together on Earth, but, even with those you have only worked with, and seen very little of socially, a link is formed which lasts. This may seem strange but the family unit on Earth does not always form the strongest links and with time its members, over here, go their own way. Whereas friends may stay together. Much depends on the strength of those links. If you think of it there is something very natural about this. If it was only earthly things that kept you together then, when they go, so does the need to be together. There is so much that is natural in this life and it is this, among other things, which gives it its charm. Well, we progress, but are we any nearer making you understand what we are on about? It would be very handy if you could ask me questions. In that way we could find out just what you have taken in.

Let us think for a moment about what I have said so far. No death, no judgement day, but no easy let out for the sinner either. Does this help you at all, this knowledge? I hope so. I hope the point is now being reached when you are thinking of changing your life style so as to meet the needs of your soul in the hereafter and not just your body in the here! Jokes apart, if you consider, after reading so far, that you should nge your outlook please do so for you cannot start too soon the job or getting your soul fit and well for its journey home. Coming home for you is a joy but for those left behind a time of sorrow. We have said this before but it is worth saying again, for it is a very important time for the one going home. It can also be a time of much stress for those left behind unless it is clearly understood what has happened. It is right that the bereaved should be comforted. For no matter how long the association has been there is usually this deep sense of loss. If the people concerned do not believe that there is life after death then this sense of loss can be very terrible indeed. At a time like this someone has to know the answer and be firm about giving it. Then the suffering can be kept to a minimum, both for the bereaved and the departed soul.

Now if you are beginning to accept what I say as being true, you will see how all this suffering is needless, in fact, you could say down right wicked and should not be allowed. None of us like partings, even when we know that it will only be for a time. If we know that the one departing is going to be much better off in every way then we must be glad for them. Not just put a brave face on it but be really glad and really happy for them. In some parts of the world this is a fact and people are, but in most other parts of the world it is a very solemn moment indeed. And as we have said before a lot of this can be put down to ignorance. Even now that you know the truth you would not be seen happy and smiling at a funeral would you? No, custom dies hard and you would be afraid of what others think, but, you know, someone has got to make a start. It really is a pity that your Church people will not come to terms with the truth and give you all a lead in this matter, for it is the time when they could really be useful. All this you are going to know for yourself one day but what satisfaction am I going to get from saying 'I told you so' for then it will be too late. You will not have spent time helping yourself and others to get ready for your big day and a fine chance if missed. Will you now, begin to get yourself ready, and at the same time talk to others about it. Start to look forward to the wonderful life ahead. You hear people say that they do not want to grow old. Well, tell them that you have had it on good authority that they do not. It is the body that becomes old and worn out. Just as soon as you arrive here you are your true self again, a young woman or a young man. 'Cheer up' some people say, 'you will soon be dead!' Cheer up and know that that is the best thing that can happen to you.

Chapter 12

What does that mean, wait and see. As I have said before it is not going to help you much if you do not believe what I am telling you. Then you arrive here to find that everything I have told you is true. So much of life is wasted because people must experience things for themselves. Up to a point experience must be gained for onself that is true, there are times however when advice from others will help you to gain experience without the useless pitfalls. My advice is the type in question. How can the average person gain the experience I have now gained? They cannot. It is sense therefore to listen to me and, for your own good, believe. The experience I have had and told you about is the kind the average person can expect to have. I can say with due modesty that I was, for most of my time on Earth, an average kind of chap so if you can say the same then you will receive the same kind of passing that I had. If you are a lady that goes for you as well. I am not going to plug Spiritualism here but if, after what you have read, you would like to join the movement then it could help you. At least it would put you in touch with like-minded people and you may find that you have spiritual gifts that can be developed. The person writing this book is such a one. He did not know he had this gift until he was told about it in Church. That was not the beginning and end of it, as you have been told, but it did get him thinking along the right lines so that when the time came for him to start to be used, he was ready. It is a wonderful story really and I am sure that he will not mind me telling it at a later date. For the moment we must continue our self-imposed job of getting you to really believe. They say that if one keeps on about a thing, then like water on a stone one can wear down the opposition. That is what I want to do with your doubts.

Doubts are the most shocking things, they can catch you at odd moments when you are off guard but they must be repulsed with certainty. Certainty is positive, doubt is negative. So you must be positive. You must say to yourself, I do accept what is written in this book, for it makes sense. It has a ring of truth about it. They say 'truth will out'. Well in this book it is out. Then you can say I believe God loves us because Jesus told us so. Many others have said the same thing. So if God loves us he cannot just do that for the short time we are on Earth. He must have other plans. He cannot just let us die and that is the end. So you will with simple logic, come to believe that life goes on when it leaves the body and that life is the real you. Then you will say, why should this chap, who is in the World of Spirit, bother to write all this unless he genuinely wanted to help? Why should he say all this if it were not true? You will find it very hard to find an answer that is not the correct one, that I truly want to help. Because as you will find out when you arrive here, help is what we all want to give and it is given in love. This is the story of the Good Samaritan that Jesus talked about. It is God's love for us and our love for him. He wants us to love our neighbour and love is about help where it is needed. So you see it cannot be odd if I want to help you, if it is God's wish. Think about it.

Chapter 13

Now the New Life. That is as good a way of starting this chapter as any, for it sums up what you are in for, when the time comes for your passing. Jesus said you should always be ready for you never know when your call may come and, as always, He is right. I have been asked, many times, since I have been over here to tell people, still on the Earth Plane, what I now know about Jesus. The first and most important thing is to confirm that He is and was what He said, during His short time on Earth. The Son of God, and therefore the Jews made their biggest mistake in having Him put to death. If He had been allowed to live He would have gone on teaching and in the end, been accepted by all as the Son of God, and the world would have become a better place for it. But man has free will and He was put to death and the plans made by God were thwarted. Oh yes, this is so, so do not throw up your hands in horror. God's plans are being thwarted, on the Earth Plane, all the time. That is why the quality of life there is so poor, compared with over here, where His word is obeyed. You cannot have it both ways you know. The people on the Earth Plane, today, who think they are being clever when they say that Jesus was not the Son of God but just a very good medium, are doing themselves and the people they convince a very great disservice. It is bad enough that Jews deny Him, but when so called Christians also do it, that is real folly as they will all come to learn in time. For the Jews, in particular, when they arrive over here and find out what a wonderful Gift God had given them, and how they threw it away and rejected it, their grief is great. There are some who teach that the Crucifixion had to be, that it was part of God's Plan. This is absolute nonsense. God would not have a plan such as that. No, the Jews at that time wanted Jesus put to death and the way the Romans carried this out, at that time, was by Crucifixion. As simple as that. If the Jews, had accepted Him, and many of them did but were afraid to come out into the open at that time, then God's Plans for the world would have flourished but man made his choice and it was the wrong one. You are all suffering for this but especially the Jews. The sins of the fathers if you like.

I will also confirm that Jesus ascended into the Spirit World, as recorded in the Bible, and that the reason why His body was found to be missing from the tomb, was that it had dematerialised. Your scientists are nearing the truth when they make their findings known about the shroud of Turin. This shroud was indeed the one used when Jesus was taken from the Cross. There are those who think it smart to debunk the story of Jesus and His death but on the whole it is true. The fact that some of the times and dates, given in the Bible, are out does not matter. People should remember how it was written. No. the facts are that Jesus was the Son of God. That He came to Earth to teach people how to lead a better life there and to prepare themselves for the life to come. That was the love of God for you all. He was trying to make things better for His children on Earth and they chose to turn Him down. That is it in a nutshell.

Now let us consider the question of Jesus being left to die on the Cross. Twice He asked His Father if this bitter cup could be taken from Him and both times the answer was no. The thing was that the situation had been taken out of God's Hands by the Jews. There was no way of reaching them spiritually. They were not prepared to listen to their inner selves when God would have told them not to do it. They were afraid that Jesus was going to undermine their power over the people and they wished to do away with Him, Then again, the crowd turned against Him because he would not pronounce Himself King. A shocking state of affairs and all because man would not listen to the simple truth that Jesus taught. Love God and one another and live a good life so that your soul would be in the best possible condition for its journey to the next world. No, they wanted pomp and show and above all they wanted Jesus to take revenge on the Romans and all in authority over them. Typical man, always wanting what was not best for him and not listening to the good advice offered to him. It was so then and it would be the same today. Are you sure the mob would not call for the release of Barabbas today as they did then? The World is very material minded today as it was then. It is more advanced scientifically, more sophisticated, but spiritually it is just as backward as it was two thousand years ago. There were those who believed Jesus, just as today but how many and who, listens to them? Do they have any power in the land, your religious leaders? There are some religious leaders who have taken power and are very busy using it for death and destruction. What kind of religion is that, that is based on hate? Can they really think they are doing God's bidding? They are very misguided. Never fear, God loves them just as he loves all mankind whatever their faults, but they will all have to suffer for the things they have done. That is the law here and in the World of Spirit. God rules supreme. 'Justice is mine' saith the Lord, 'I will repay.'

There I will leave this subject but you must read into it the underlying theme of this book. There is no death and nothing changes when you pass over. You are what you are, but you can start now to help your soul to get into better shape for your big day, if only you will accept what I am telling you. Do not fear, we are all God's children and He wants us all to succeed. There is nothing that cannot be done to help you, if only you will ask for it, but the first step must be taken by you. This is the Law. You have freewill, remember, so the onus is yours. 'Ask and ye shall receive.' There are so many things you have been advised to do. You read them and take not the slightest notice of them. What can we do with you? There is now the question of your wanting to be helped. Just as some people will not listen, there are those who will. As I have already said, there is never too much trouble to be taken over those who need help and ask for it. Most people outside the spirit movement do not realise that they have spirit Helpers with them most of their waking life, but they do. These dedicated souls try, as best they can, to watch over you and keep you out of needless trouble. When you ask for help they are your first line of communication. They do what they can and obtain help themselves if they need it. Most of the impressions you receive come from them. As when you cannot think how help has come in the shape of an answer you have received or something has saved you from an accident. Ideas and thoughts come into your head from your Helpers. During sleep, much help can be given to you.

You should use this time to help you with your problems. Think about them before you go to sleep and by the morning you may either have the answer or you will find that you feel much better about it and the worry is not as great. Your Helper will have been talking to you and will have been able to reassure you. You see, although the body sleeps the soul is very much awake and will be able to talk to your Helper. Some people are lucky enough to remember; they have recall, most do not, but you do have a feeling, an impression, which is a help. Quite a few people, though not all, are able to leave their bodies during the sleep state and indulge in what is known as astral travel.

The soul leaves the body but is still connected by a very fine cord. When you pass over for good, then it is this cord that breaks. If you are one of the lucky ones who can do this then you have a very entertaining time for you are able to travel at will and can meet all your friends and those who have passed over.

There are places in the Spirit World that you do not visit but you see enough to give you a good idea of what awaits you in due time. The fact that most people cannot remember what they have been doing is a pity, but it cannot be helped. Sometimes you may just remember a flash and you think it was a dream. If your memory is of a bright sunny place with lots of colour, perhaps a garden, then the chances are you have remembered part of your visit. Some say that if you remembered what the Spirit World was like you would not go back to Earth. This is not so. The soul knows what it must do because it is still attached to the body by that cord and if anything happens, such as a noise to waken the body up, then the soul is back like a shot. This can leave you feeling a bit put out and flustered when you awake with a start but no real damage is done, and you soon settle down. You will gather from this that those who are able to leave their bodies in this manner, can receive quite a lot of education of the soul which will stand them in good stead later on. The fact that the body knows nothing about it does not matter much although, if you did, it would soon convert you into being a believer.

What else can I tell you about this astral travel? Not very much, for the big thing is to have the ability to let the soul leave the body. Once this has been mastered, what it does with its freedom is up to it or you, if you prefer. Friends will meet and talk to you, that seems to be the most popular pastime. The soul will always leave the body during sleep state but in most cases will just stay a foot or so above. It will not get up and go unless it wants to. Free will again you see. If your Helpers are able to contact the soul at this stage then away it will go. More I cannot tell you. I can well believe you think this is a strange business but then playing the violin can be until you know how. True? We must try and take the mystery out of all this but frankly I see this as a tall order. There must be a mystery until you know how the trick is done. But you can talk about it and wonder about it until the trick becomes an every day thing. That is the only way for you to prepare your soul for passing. Keep on thinking about it. Do not push it away, make it a natural part of your present life, so that you will start to live the way that is best for your soul. That, you must realise by now, is what your present life is all about.

Chapter 14

Superstition is another strange thing. Why are most people superstitious? It is a hangover from the time when the world did not know God. It was worshipping idols that it came about and yet people still believe in superstitions and practice them. Not a very complimentary thing to do in this enlightened age, to put yourself back to those dark ages before God was brought into our lives. God has got to live in your heart if you are going to make a good preparation for your passing. If you do this you will start to live the life He wants for you. It will become 'His will' as you pray. You are asking for this in your prayer but, in fact, do nothing yourself to help this state to come about. Why we cannot think. I know I was as bad as the rest when I was on the Earth Plane but now I know better and it is for this reason that I am telling you to work, yourself, towards bringing about God's Will on earth. You think I am asking too much of you. You think the weight of world opinion is against you. You are wrong. There are plenty of people on the Earth Plane who are working for this. They shine out like beacons for us to see, and we over here give them all the help we can. What is God's Will? He wants us all to be happy and He wants us to help each other attain this state. He wants each of us to share in the good things he has provided for us, not just the few. But above all He wants us to stop worshipping man made things and start glorying in the things He has given us. Only in this way can God's Will be done on Earth. His Will can only be the right one and surely man should be able to see this. Surely man should stop and think about this instead of thinking it is his own will that must prevail.

Look around your world today and see what a fine old mess man has made of it by insisting that his will, not God's, should be done. Just point to one spot on Earth that is trouble free. You will have a job. You know in your hearts that this is so and you know that your soul is sick of it all. There are times when you feel this more strongly than others. You are heartily sick of all the man made trouble that you see, hear about or read about. 'Why', you cry 'must this state of things be?'

And you know the answer all the time. It is man exerting his material power to get his own way, his will, that is causing it all. And because there is no universal justice in it, it must fail in the end. You can see it all around you. Man forcing his own will on others, not for their good, for his own. God's Will is not like that. His Will is born out of love for us all and not as man's is, out of greed for a few such as family or himself. This short sighted approach by man does not have to be accepted by all. It is true, in the broad sense, that you cannot do much about it physically but you can do plenty about it spiritually. You can pray that strength will be given to those in high places who can see what God wants for us. Given this strength, this help, they will be able to change things.

Prayer is a strong force and can help. Give these leaders, who, you know, are really working for your good, which is God's will, all the help you can with your prayers. Really think about them and send out your thoughts for their success. They need all the strength you can give them, just as you need the good things their strength can bring about. Never be afraid of opening your heart in prayer. We know it is not the easiest of things to do. but if you will just talk to God as you would to a friend on the Earth Plane, that is the best way to start. The other thing is keep it simple. Do not try and think up special phrases or sentences as your religious leaders tend to do. No, just talk or think normally. We know it would be a lot easier for some people if the talking or thinking were not so one sided but in your present state of development this is the best that can be done for you. Just pray and know that you are doing nothing but good. Then again you wonder how long you should go on praying and how many different things you shold pray for. Given the present state of the world, we agree, your scope is limitless. Many people are praying all day long and sometimes without realising it. Going about your daily work you are thinking about things and people and very often they are calls for help. Perhaps you pass someone in the street and you think 'poor soul', well it is a loving thought and that is prayer. We can go on giving examples, but we think you know what we mean. Some make a point of saying 'God Bless You' when they see a blind person, a cripple or someone in distress. This is a good practice and if more people were to do it, and mean it, it would help to make the world a better place. Loving thoughts are always welcome for they do everyone good. The sender and the receiver, both. They also create a better atmosphere.

Some people who are really sensitive can pick up these atmospheres only too well and they will tell you how wonderful a peaceful and loving atmosphere is and how unpleasant the other kind can be. Others who are sensitive, can see little pin pricks of light or stars and sometimes colour. Those who understand, know that they are loving thoughts, sent to them from the World of Spirit. They are comforting thoughts and if you say thank you, then the sender will know they have been received. There is a chance that you may see these lights and not realise it. They are usually at an angle from you, not straight on, rather out of the corner of your eye. Down and to your right might be a better way of putting it. But whether you see these lights or not, you may rest assured that loving thoughts are being sent to you from those you know who are now in spirit. Perhaps you see them and wonder what they are. They are thought waves that we use, over here, to let people know that we are on our way to see them. In your case they are thoughts that are sent to you to cheer you up. They do not always get through to you because your own thoughts may be too strong at the time. That is why, if you can, you should sit quietly, during the day, and let our thoughts come to you. How will you know the difference between your thoughts and ours? That is a good question and I am afraid I do not have the answer but if you try, at the same time each day, you will, after a time, find that you are given messages and that you will become aware of the difference between the two types of thought. It is done in the same way that this book is being written.

Although the hand is being controlled by our friend's Father, we are able to impress upon his mind the words we wish to write. So we are able to have his full cooperation. During this time thoughts of his own are taking place and there are times when he thinks one word will follow but we use another. This, plus the fact that the hand is controlled soon lets him know that we are deciding what will be written and not he. To begin with he was not too sure about all this but now he is. Also he has been worried that what we say will not make sense to you. Well, we can assure him on that point for this book has already been written over here, and we have been over it many times to make sure that it is readable and understandable. What happens after the Earth writing is finished, is that he goes through it for spelling and other mistakes. then, at times, words are left out but other than that the book is ready to go to the printer after it has been accepted by a publisher. We tell you all this for we think you will be interested. We are about halfway through the book at this stage, so you see we have plenty to talk about.

We think this is a very different book from those you have been used to. It is a style we have developed, my sister and I, and we hope you like it. I know we keep repeating things but how else can we get our points over? We have however tried to talk and reason with you and not just say 'That's it, get on with it.' We are so anxious, for your sake, that you should accept what we have to tell you. If we are really able to get our message across to all who read this book then we shall indeed have achieved something. Quite certainly there are people on the Earth Plane who are going to knock it saying it is all the work of our 'friend'. On the other hand there will be those who will be favourably impressed and the end result will be that the book will be given plenty of publicity and a lot of people will read it. We welcome criticism for it gives us a chance to answer whatever may be said. Our friend who is writing this on the Earth Plane says he is not looking forward to this part of his work but we will be with him, to help him, and the answers he must give will be given in the same way as this has been written. He will have to do quite a bit of travelling but he is used to that. We can see all this and are telling you in advance what will happen. You can then see for yourself as you read that it really is not our friend on the Earth Plane who is writing it. We can tell you a lot more about what will happen when this book comes out and this will help our readers to believe that it truly was written in the Spirit World in the first instance.

Chapter 15

The Summerland is what you may call this wonderful World of Spirit. Some places on the Earth Plane boast that they have Summer all the year round, but really they have their tongues in their cheeks. Here there are no tongues in cheek. The Spirit climate is perfect. Like all that God controls it is everything that is best for the soul. On the Earth Plane you have conditions that are most suited to man. You may not always appreciate it if the summer is wet and cold, but that is the climate you have and it changes all the time, here it never changes. We never tire of it as perhaps you might think. The fact that it is always the same is accepted by us just as you accept yours. The reason is that Spirit needs this kind of atmosphere to live in because it is spirit. 'Yes', you say, 'I can believe this', for there are times when you seem to know when the truth is being given to you. Much of this has to do with the fact that the soul leaves the body, as we have already told you, and it has seen all this for itself. So when you are told it, the soul remembers. Think what a joy it is for the soul to live in an atmosphere like this. What a wonderful life you have ahead of you, and what a pity some spoil it by arriving over here with the soul in an unfit state, brought about by selfish unloving lives. We have said all this before and we shall be saying it again. In fact we cannot drum it in sufficiently. People on the Earth Plane forget so easily. They read something or hear it and say 'yes that is right, that is what I must do.' But something happens and all that good resolve goes by the board.

You know very well that the simple unselfish life is best for you, and you are determined to live it until you come into contact with someone doing the opposite and you think 'why should I go without if they do not'. So your good resolve is gone. Do not let other people decide how you live. If you want to you can lead the kind of life that is good for you, even when all around are doing the other thing. You know you can be yourself and other people will admire you for it. Too often today, especially among the young, things are done that run absolutely contrary to their nature, but they do them because they are afraid of

61

being left out of the crowd. What a pity it is that they cannot be told that if the crowd do not want them for themselves, then it is best not to be in it. Like attracts like and they are happy with each other, the good and the bad. The trouble always sets in when someone tries to make themselves what they are not. We are quite sure that a lot of the young who finish up on drugs would not do so if this simple truth was taught them. Do not try and join in with people you really are not happy with. In time they will meet up with people they will want to be with. They should be taught to spend their energy on this rather than the effort of trying to fit in where they should not be. If you could see the pitiful state of these young people when they pass over much more would be done than is already being done, to teach them to stay away from drugs and to help them come off them, before it is too late. For they are not passing in the normal way. Dead they are, but they have taken their own lives and this, as we have said before, is the last thing you want to do.

The Summerland is the place to which you are all heading, regardless of the way you choose to take. As you may remember, we told you that you would be met, when your time comes to pass over. And this is indeed so. You will be met by someone you know very well. Someone that you are pleased to see and happy to go with. This person is chosen from among your friends and relations by the group you are to join. When you pass over you become their special responsibility. While on Earth they have kept an eye on you but now you are in Spirit they are able to have an even stronger influence on you. You should be happy about this for, as we have said before, you really are among friends who think only of your best interest. Strange, you may think, that there can be such people for on the Earth Plane you do not come across this very much, but then that is because you are in a material situation where one is encouraged to look after oneself. 'You have got to look after yourself' people say, and up to a point this is true, but not to the exclusion of all else. If you do you become selfish and self centred and this is bad for your soul. People on the earth Plane are, in the main, only too willing to help each other, especially if someone is in trouble, and that is the love for your neighbour of which Jesus spoke. In this Summerland, where all are so happy, love is the driving force and it comes to us from God. He is Love and when all around are loving and caring then you can really let yourself go and be happy with them for you know that nothing is going to come along and spoil it. If only this could be so on the Earth Plane.

It could, but you see there are so many selfish influences at work there, so many people looking after themselves which usually means at the expense of others. Then there are those in a position of power who can and do, make life difficult for those working under them. You know all this as well as we do. Over here there is none of that. We have people in a position of power, for wherever you go you always find that there is someone above you, but these people are put over us to help and to guide. They are put in this position because they are very evolved souls who have been over here a very long time, and have gained experience which makes them fit for the position. Not a son of someone or a friend who has been given a leg up. No, that just cannot happen here, and we must admit that some souls who arrive are rather put out when they find this to be so. Especially if their church has led them to believe otherwise. Here the new soul is like a new born baby and has just about as much say in the running of things as one would on the Earth Plane. Meakness is a very fitting condition for the new soul to arrive in. But then Jesus taught that two thousand years ago, among other things. Well, we are getting on with our guide to the Hereafter and we hope that what you are being told is going to stick. Chances are you will have to read it again, if you are new to this way of thinking. It may be too much for you to take in at first. Even myself, when I first arrived here, could not really believe it and I had been in the Spiritualist movement for many years and thought I knew something about it. It is all so different from what we had been led to believe. Or was it that we were never really told. That could have been it. A lot of talking goes on but at the end of it all you are none the wiser. Certainly I cannot remember being told even what we have told you so far. We are always told that there is no death and are usually given a few tips as to how we should behave, but not much on the practical part of leaving one life and starting the other. Well, with luck you will know a lot more by the end of this book. Do I sound an odd kind of chap to you? In a way I am. I always had a sense of humour that perhaps took a bit of getting used to and naturally, being a part of the true me, it has come over here with me.

So now let us talk a little more about Summerland. Every time I think of the years spent on the Earth Plane I marvel at the way the soul puts up with it, when it knows what life can really be like. People go on thinking that their life on Earth is the thing when all the time they are having to put up with a very second best, and now I am talking of most of the people of the West, who enjoy a good standard of living.

True there are plenty who are not, but compared to the standards of some people of the so called Third World they are doing very well. Think then how surprised these people are when they arrive over here. They have their own reception area and their own friends to meet them but after they have settled down they mix in with other souls who have reached the same stage of development. There is no other segregation. The state of your soul decides the company you keep. What about language? Well, as I said before, they have their own areas just as on the Earth Plane, but there is nothing to stop them travelling if the state of the soul allows it. There are plenty of well developed or advanced souls outside the West as you can well imagine and communication between souls such as this is not a problem. Please remember it is in the soul's best interest for it to be in the company of those that suit it best. They are then happy and contented. At all stages there are teachers and helpers who will help the soul to advance when it is ready, and when it is ready it will want to. That is how it works, free will always, never any pressure brought to bear. When the soul is ready to move on it will know. Until that time it is impossible for it to move from the area it is in. This is a natural law which is perfect. When all souls are of a like kind or state of development then there is perfect peace and harmony. We think you can understand that and perhaps approve of it. If people arrive here and for some reason or other are not going to get along with others, then they do not meet until the soul likely to cause the trouble has had time to settle down and come to realise what this life is all about. We keep on telling you that you arrive here exactly as you are with all your habits good and bad. Now there is nothing new about this. People can be good or bad friends on Earth. They can be the same here. If one or the other persists in this then they just do not meet, until they come to their senses. Trouble over here as you know it is non-existent.

We suppose jealousy is about the biggest trouble maker and that is a state that the soul must be cleansed of. Most other causes of trouble disappear because they are based on material things but jealousy is of the soul and has to be got rid of before the soul can take its place with others. Our very best advice to anyone on the Earth Plane who suffers from jealousy is to overcome it before they come here. Really it is all in the mind and it must be faced up to. It should not be mistaken for envy, though sometimes it is. Envy is material in a sense and not nearly as bad. Anyway there is nothing to be envious of over here, but jealousy is terrible. It must be paid for, and it is painful if left to be treated over here. So people with jealous natures must really work at it, in their own best interest, so that they have a clean bill of health. Naturally over here the Helper dealing with such a one will do so with love and understanding having perhaps been through it themselves, but the soul must suffer until it is jealous no more. That is enough about that but if you know of people who have this kind of nature it is your duty to tell them what they are in for if they do not change their ways.

Chapter 16

People who think about Life After Death, as you put it, think of themselves as going into a sleep state from which they are awakened by someone or something when the time has come for them to be judged. This quaint idea will not stand up if you give it a little thought. How can the thousands and thousands of souls that pass over, during your day, be lined up to be judged and do you really think it is a very practical way of doing it? No, you say, it is not, and you are right. The way it really happens we have already explained. The judgement part is left to the soul itself. 'This cannot be', I hear you say, but it is. You are the Judge. Your soul arrives in the condition that you have caused it to be in through your life style. Most, we are pleased to say, arrive in pretty good shape. The colour of their souls acceptable to all who greet them. This is because most people are not bad and the things they have done are not things to hurt the soul, theirs or others. You may think that there is a lot of trouble in the world today, and you are right, but the ones causing the trouble, the evil ones, are but few, it is the ones who suffer that are the many. Your news is always full of the bad things that go on, not much is said about the good. Human nature wants it this way so that is what it gets. Over here it is the good news that everyone wants to hear so we do not have bad news because no one makes it. No robbery or violence to report. No strikes. No one doing someone else a bad service. Not a thing that is bad because the soul does not find a need for that kind of thing. It is very busy putting itself right by doing things for others or at school catching up with all the education it missed on Earth, or both. There is so much time here, as you would put it, to do everything and because you do not become tired, you can go on and on, from one thing to another if that is what you wish.

If I may speak of myself I will tell you that just now I am very busy with this book that my sister and friends are helping me with. On top of that I spend much time with my teacher for I find I have so much to learn. Then I must spend time back on the Earth Plane for I am still interested in what is going on there among my friends. My wife gives me cause for concern for she will not face up to the fact that for the time being, we are living on different planes. This is common on the part of those left behind. But it is in their best interest to accept the fact, for they cannot alter it, and they only cause unnecessary suffering to themselves and those departed. If only they would accept that the one who has passed on is so much better off and could be very happy indeed if only the loved ones, left behind, would be happy for them. Nothing changes. If there was love and gratitude, on the part of the departed one, this does not change with coming over here and is seen in even better light for the good it really is. It is recorded in the soul of the one left behind and nothing can change it. If there is love between people on the Earth Plane then when you pass over it can only grow stronger. Please never think that loved ones grow away from you with time. There is no time. There is plenty to do over here and we must do what we can, but this does not mean we are too busy to have time for the loved ones left behind. Please understand this. Please remember that suffering caused through thinking this way helps no one. Go on loving the departed one and be happy for them. Your love is welcomed and is returned ten fold and your happiness is recorded with such joy over here. So please, *please* love and be happy for the departed one, it makes such a difference to them. God blesses all who can do this so do try for both your sakes. If I sound emotional it is because I am. People think that with parting things change. They do not. The soul has left the body and cannot be seen by most people but that is all, so everything that is said and thought about the departed one is known to them. So you see, depending upon the thoughts or words the soul can be made very happy or very sad. In fact miserable, and on top of this, they usually cannot get their own thoughts over to put matters right. You can see then why it is so important to think only in terms of love and happiness.

After people have been in the Spirit World for a long time, as you call it, then they do pass on into a higher life. Their souls have developed to a degree that makes it possible for them to do this and at such a time it could be that the loved ones who have joined them in spirit are not yet ready to go forward with them but this does not make any difference for the bond between them is still there. What has changed is that both are now in Spirit and both understand the new position and, far from being sad at the parting and all the other feelings of the Earth Plane, there is now great joy for the one who is now ready to journey on. How we wish that this could be the position from the start.

If my wife and countless others could understand this and act accordingly there would be so much joy over here and the link between loved ones made much stronger.

We all have to face up to the fact there are those with whom we cannot get on on the Earth Plane and for a time it is the same over here but as you progress in this new life your soul and other's change. You become better and better spiritually through your work, your schooling and the atmosphere that you are in. You are made very much aware of God and that He loves you and everyone else and that His greatest wish is for us all to live in happiness and peace together. Knowing this how can we do other than carry out His wishes? That is why life over here is so wonderful. No one is trying to do anything other than be helpful. No one is trying to be better, or worse, thinking they are better. No, this does not arise for you all know that you are with people of like development and that service to others is the best thing for your soul. This must be done with love and pleasure, it is no good to you if you make it a chore. Anyway if you did it would be picked up by the one being helped and the help would be rejected. Only the good in everthing is accepted over here. The one who pretends to help gets nowhere and so, in this way, the lesson is brought home to them. We go on and on learning for as we master one thing we are invited to try another but always within our capabilities, never forced and always if we choose so to do.

Now to discuss other things. What do you think happens to all the souls who cannot accept what has happened to them? They will not allow themselves to be brought over here when they pass so they stay on the Earth Plane. There are very many such souls and to you they are Earth bound. They are for us a never ending cause of worry. Not that they can do themselves any real harm, it is just that they are so unhappy with their lot. They can cause trouble on the Earth Plane if they use the power they have to move things about, and they frighten people with the things they get up to. You should not worry about them but you can pray for them and ask that they will allow their spirit helpers to take them away. We can do nothing for them if they do not ask for help. They are a law unto themselves for as long as they wish to be. Usually this state of affairs comes about by an accident or other untimely death where the passing is not planned. When the soul is not met by someone they know and love who can guide them they do not realise that they are dead. Thie is the problem, for, in most cases, they have no true idea of what death is all about and anyway they still feel very much alive, so how can they be dead? They are in a tricky situation. As we have said before there is nothing new that can happen so there are helpers who are trained to look after souls like this and they are never given up for lost. Sooner or later the truth will be brought home to them and the Helper will be rewarded for all his efforts by witnessing the happiness the soul exudes when he is brought home to be among his own at last.

Let us now talk about Spirit Healing. For most of you this has got to be an abstract thing for you see nothing happening, and the chances are that you feel nothing. Spirit Healing is not even easy for us over here to understand. The spirit Doctors are highly evolved souls and have been training for a long time before they are allowed to practice on their own. Healing Guides work under the Doctors and are given limited responsibility. There have many famous spirit Doctors working through mediums on the Earth Plane over the years, and this will go on for as long as they are needed. Healing is given all the time to many people without them knowing it. It is not always necessary for a Healer on the Earth Plane to be there but more healing power can be concentrated when they are. What makes a Healer? Well, what makes a medium? It is their ability to be used as an instrument or channel. Something in their make-up which is called sensitivity is the thing. If they are sensitive and sympathetic they can be used but they must be willing to do this work. It is unfortunate more people do not realize they can be used in this way for a great deal of good work can be done. Lots of people will not accept spirit healing and this is a pity, for help has been given to many over the years and much suffering has been alleviated by the spirit world during this time. We here are all aware of the sickness on the Earth Plane. Much of it is caused by bad eating and drinking habits. When the body is young it can get away with it but as you grow older it catches up with you. Also the mind can give the body a lot of trouble by upsetting the harmony which is so necessary if all component parts are to work properly. The healing power from Spirit is a balm which will put the harmony back. We never say that you should not go to your doctor on the Earth Plane. We say you should, but there are times when your doctor will say he can do nothing for you and then you turn to spirit. Sometimes this is also too late. What we say is go to your doctor and at the same time have spirit healing. The two can work together. What is it that stops one going for spirit healing we wonder.

Let us talk about that. Most people think that there is something

69

unnatural about it and perhaps a bit wrong, just as they think Spiritualism is wrong, and that speaking to departed souls is wrong. In fact *they* are wrong. Spirit healing is the most natural thing in your life. It comes from God and must be right for all. You cannot argue this point for it is a fact. The greatest spirit healer of all times was Jesus and He is the Son of God. With this in mind do you think it unreasonable if we say that spirit healing can only be good for you? That it is the most natural of all healing. and that this, together with a far better understanding of herbs and their uses, would be a great help to your medical people. I was used as a healer when I was on the Earth Plane and I know now that I was able to do more good than I thought at the time, owing to the fact that most of us cannot see the healing rays at work and the person receiving them does not always feel the degree of improvement that has taken place. But from here I am able to see what has been done and I want to say that if those who came to me will only carry on healing with another healer they will improve. You know that most healing takes time. This is perhaps another reason why people will not go to spirit healers but they are wrong again. Jesus was a very powerful healer, as we read in the Bible, but most healing is not of that nature. Some of our Earth healers have had spectacular results but in the main spirit healing is a slow business. If you accept this and use it together with your doctor then you will be in good hands. Spirit healing for me is a wonderful thing and I mean just that, it is full of wonder. If you could see healers at work you would say the same.

There is so much colour used. Different colours for different treatments. Then there are the wonderful souls who are seeing to the treatment. Their colours are brilliant and add to the picture. Quite different from the drab little rooms your doctors use. But then to be truthful the Earth Plane is drab after this World of Spirit. So use spirit healers if you need them and know that they are only too happy to help you. Do not think it is unnatural, not after all I have told you. I like to think that, after reading this book, you will find out where your nearest Spiritualist Church is and go to a Service. It could be that you will be told that you can be used for healing, just as the one was told who is writing this book on the Earth Plane for me. He has not much faith but nevertheless he is able to give healing to his wife and it is doing her a lot of good, slowly, yes, but the power is working. If you can be used by the Spirit World you will be, it does not matter if you are a 'doubting Thomas' like my friend here, the spirit power will pass through you.

Remember that it is not you who gives the healing. That comes from God and the spirit healers do what is necessary. You are the instrument through which they are able to channel the power. It may be a long time before you need it and it is my hope that you never do. But, should the time come, then use this gift from God that can only be for your good.

Chapter 17

I will now tell you about your Aura. This is your spiritual clothing, during the time you are on the Earth Plane. The body looks after the soul, in as much that it lives within it. The Earth Plane is material and the soul needs a material covering so as to live. The Aura is the spiritual part of you that can be seen by those who are gifted with spirit sight. Much is claimed and much is misunderstood about this phenomenon by people on the Earth Plane. They read into it things that are not there. They talk about it as if it has some spiritual importance, whereas it has none. They say it can tell you about the soul, what it is going to be during its time on Earth or what it could be, given the chance. This is not so either. The Aura will reflect the state of the soul, at any given time, just as your face lights up when you are happy or tears fall when you are sad, or become red in the face when you are angry, and so on. But having said that, that is all there is to it, the real you is the soul. The colour of the soul is the true state of your spiritual being. This fact does not mean that the Aura is of no importance. It is, in as much, that other souls who see it, during the time the soul is on Earth, can recognize it by its colouring at that time for what it is, just as you recognize a person with your material eye. People wear different clothes at different times, but as long as you can see the face, the head or the general body shape you know who they are. That is what the Aura does for the spirit eye and that is about it, in a nutshell.

Let us now talk of something new for a change. Let us talk about you. How can we do this, you say, when we do not know each other? True, but we all have so much in common, you would be surprised at how much people do know about each other. There is a thing on the Earth Plane known as psychometry. This is the ability to tell others something of their past, by holding a personal object belonging to the person in question. A watch, a ring, keys, anything that has been kept on the person for sometime and has, therefore picked up vibrations from them. Some are better at this than others. Much depends on how sensitive the one is who gives the demonstration. When on the Earth

Plane I was quite good at this but I did not really understand what I was doing. I would hold the object I was given and in a little while I would find that thoughts would come into my head and I would pass these thoughts on to the person concerned. They would be things that on their own, meant nothing to me, but to the person I was talking to they did. This always seemed good proof to me that the supernatural was at work. Now I know what it is all about, I am not surprised about it all. We have already said that, good and bad, all things are recorded by the soul. The way the recording is made is by vibrations, for want of a better word, and these vibrations are also collected, in part, by objects that are kept on the person. Some people, mediums, have this sensitivity developed to a very high degree and not only know things but also receive pictures in their mind. Vibrations stay in the place where people have lived out their lives. Here again the medium sensitive enough to do so, can tune in and give a good account of what has happened there. You perhaps have walked into a room for the first time, and have said what a nice atmosphere there was. You are picking up vibrations and they are pleasing ones. Other places you do not like and this time you are picking up the unpleasant kind. Generally, however, you will pick up nothing, neither good nor bad vibrations, these are just normal and not strong enough for you to sense.

There are many people who say they can judge character. They feel something from the person concerned and that they like them, or that there is something wrong and they do not. Usually what they are picking up are the thought vibrations given out by the other person. Just as there are those who tend to do all the talking on the Earth Plane, there are those who tend to listen. It is the same with the spirit side of your nature, and therefore there are some who tend to send out their thought waves and others who tend to sit back and receive them. Now a word of warning here. The thoughts sent out by those on the Earth Plane are often coloured by material things, in fact it would be correct to say that most of them are, and therefore they cannot be said to be a true indication of character. You may say that a good character cannot send out bad thought waves, but this is not so and I will tell you why. A good soul is open to all the thoughts that the bad receive. They are basically the same. The difference is that one will act upon the thought and the other will reject it. The free will is there. One may choose the right, the other the left. That action is the one recorded on the soul. Now we know that Jesus taught that by thinking an act you were in fact doing it. This has not changed but he was talking to the people of the time and He needed to use strong language to impress them. Today the same pressure is there but the soul has become more sophisticated if you like, because of the life so many lead. Therefore we say the thought enters the mind through the sheer force of modern living; is considered, and accepted or rejected, and that is the part that is recorded by the soul. At the same time, however, the thought waves may have been sensed by the other person, and this is what Jesus was talking about. An impression is formed one way or another, but the final action, the one that really counts, may be something different. Have we made ourselves clear?

We have tried to explain as simply as possible but as we have said before, thoughts are very powerful things and you must, during your time on Earth, learn to control them, for over here they are picked up just as your speech is. Do not doubt this but take it as Gospel truth, as you say, and you will find that your quality of life over here is much better from the start. I did not fully understand this when I first came over so I am talking from experience. Well, that is all we have to say about you for the moment. We are constantly trying to make you think of your real self. Not the one you see in the looking glass but the real you, the soul that lives for the time being, in the body you do see. That is the part of you that endures and must be made ready for your life over here.

Chapter 18

It is wonderful here, as usual, while we write. We are sitting at a table out on the verandah of the home I am sharing with my Sister. My Sister was quite a bit older than myself, when we lived on the Earth Plane and, in lots of ways, was a Mother to me. Being quite brilliant as a writer on Earth she is a big help to me here. Why, you may ask, does she not get on with the job of writing instead of me? So she could, but I think she is indulging her kid brother, who also wanted to write during his time on Earth, but never did. Letters, yes, I wrote those and enjoyed doing so, even after I lost my sight. I would sit at my typewriter and write away, using my odd sense of humour on those who were to receive them. I could type before my sight went, so it was not difficult to carry on. One or two little things were added so that I knew where I was, but the keyboard was well known to me and a fold in the bottom of the page allowed me to feel when I was near the end. The thing that drives me on to write is the fact that although I was in the Spiritualist movement, on Earth, I was never given a clear picture of what to expect when I came over here. So, if by writing this book I can help others to understand what to expect and how to prepare for it, I will do them some good, myself some good, and I will have written my book! How about that for an achievement? Anyway I am enjoying this self-imposed task, which is more than the poor chap who is having to do the writing, over there. He will be pleased when it is finished, I think. But there is more writing to come, when this is finished, so he can cheer up.

Well, as I have said, it is a wonderful day here as always and we are feeling very happy with our lot, and it is this that we wish we could share with all of you on the Earth Plane. Perhaps we should tell you a little more about the house we live in. It is a single storey bungalow with a verandah running most of the way round and a little terrace overlooking the garden. The garden is a thing of beauty by itself. It is not very large but there is quite a lot of grass with flower borders on both sides of the lawn that runs down to a stream at the bottom. There are trees and shrubs dotted about and the colour and the scent is wonderful. Bees, birds and butterflies are everywhere and the birds especially are something. There are all kinds you could wish for. All singing away, and in the background the bees in the flowers nearby with the sound of a fountain playing, round the corner, out of sight of where I am sitting. All this has to make one happy.

Did I tell you about my friend who comes to call on me from time to time? He has been over here much longer than myself and is quite advanced. We knew one another when we were on the Earth Plane. I worked for him, as his secretary, for quite some time and strong links were formed then. He was not interested in Spiritualism although I did talk to him about it. This fact does not seem to have made any difference to his progress over here. He had a normal passing, which got him away to a good start, but he was a good, kind man when he was on the Earth Plane and had no trouble settling down over here. So much depends on this. Here he goes again, you will say, but it is true, and we cannot say it to you too often. If you wish to enjoy this new life, right from the beginning, make sure your soul is in the best possible condition when it arrives here. My friend has just arrived so the writing will have to stop for a while.

Later and my friend has gone. He had some sad news to tell. One of his grandsons had had a car accident and was in hospital on the Earth Plane. He had been to see him and he was so near passing that he had recognised him. We do hope he will remember this when he is better. The sad thing is we know the suffering this poor lad will have to go through before he is well. If you could see all the friends who gather at hospitals, from the Spirit World, you would be rather surprised. If anything there are more people from here, than from Earth. Healers, friends and those who have come to take the soul home, are all there and there is plenty of coming and going all the time. We are always advised when you have trouble on the Earth Plane, and help arrives from here at once. Our main concern is for those who are about to pass over so that they can be met and their new state explained to them so that their passing may become as natural as possible despite the way it happened. So many people say they are not afraid of death, just the nature of it. Up to a point they have something. If the passing comes after much suffering then the soul has been through a bad time and the passing at the end of such a time is a great relief. But, as I have said before in the actual passing there is no pain at all. Can we go further and say that death is a real friend to those who have painful ailments and who do not want to go on. The doctor who helps the soul to pass at such a time is doing nothing wrong in the sight of God. If the doctor can satisfy himself that there is nothing further that can be done for the body then it should not be kept going, for it is keeping the soul a prisoner for nothing. I do not speak lightly on this point, and it is not I who am speaking. I have taken advice from the best possible source open to me, and I have been told that the sin lies in keeping people alive, and in pain, not in helping them to pass when their time has come. God never wants us to suffer. He does not cause it, man does. If you look into all situations where trouble is to be found you will see man's hand in it. People call on God, to help them out of the trouble that man has gone to a lot of trouble to create.

God does not work like that. When I was on the Earth Plane I could never understand why God let things happen and I am sure you have done the same. Now I am a little wiser. God has given man free will. He has given man a choice. If this was not so man could learn nothing on the Earth Plane at all. If man is wise he can get along very well most of the time, but it is not long before selfishness, greed or jealousy creeps into something, and away we go. We have trouble on our hands. At that time you can ask for help but the chances are the only help you will get is to have the error of your ways pointed out to you. God loves everyone, He will not take sides. So when you are in trouble the best thing is to look it in the face and find out why. When you have the answer to this you can then ask advice as to how best to get out of it, but you must work on it yourself, not just hand it over to God, as some people think they should do. Help you can always ask for but the problem is yours. Help, in the way of advice, will always be given, but if you think that you can hand your problem over and then sit back and expect your spirit helpers to sort it out for you they will not. I was never happier when I was on the Earth Plane, than when I was giving people advice. If I could see the answer then I gave it. If I could not I said so. Now, over here, I am somewhat wiser about many things, but what stands out most, is the way man gets himself into trouble because he just will not think things through. If he would only do this he would save himself a lot of worry.

77

Chapter 19

Now we come to the time when we must talk about healing which we have touched on already but not very deeply. This is a favourite subject of mine, used as I was for healing when I was on the Earth Plane. You should know that the person used for healing is but the instrument through which the spirit people work. If you can be used for healing it shows up in your Aura and, in this way, you are worked upon until you are suitable. If you are a Spiritualist, it will not be long before you will be told of this fact and then it is left to you whether you become a healer or not from a practical point of view. If you are a suitable subject, and do not know it, you may still be used but not to such good effect. Most healers have no formal training as such but with practice their healing guides can make them understand to which spot their hands should be moved and, as the healing power is passed through them, then the sick part of the body receives it to the best advantage. The success of healing depends on so many things. First, the Instrument. If it is truly sensitive and the healing power can pass freely through it then it can be used more successfully which is obvious. Next the nature of the complaint. If it is well established, as some are, by the time healing is given then this can also take longer. The one thing that never changes is the Power. It is there all the time. If, for some reason, it is necessary to step it up this can be arranged but healing is a gentle thing in itself. If or when there are complications the healing guide will call in a spirit doctor or surgeon. This must make sense to you. These people are specialists and will either carry out the operation, if one is necessary, or advise the Guide as to the best method of treatment. There are those, on the Earth Plane who are advanced enough to be able to see all this. They can see the cause of the trouble and they can see the specialist at work upon it. If conditions are right, the trouble can be removed by dematerialising it or by manipulation when a part of the body such as the spine, can be put right.

The spine can cause a lot of trouble to people, especially in later life and if they are overweight. The spirit doctors can administer an anaesthetic, either local or general and there are plenty of people on the Earth Plane, today who can testify to this. Some wonderful work has been done, by spirit doctors, but you do not always hear about them because by and large people do not talk about anything to do with Spirit. It is still not accepted, generally, as a normal thing. Witchcraft is how most people think of it. This will change with time, as you know. In the meantime the work of healing the sick goes on unnoticed by the majority upon the Earth Plane. This does not bother the healers, for they know what they are doing, but it would be to the advantage of people generally if they would turn for help to the Spirit World. We know that many doctors on the Earth Plane do know the value of spirit healing and are instruments themselves, but again, they cannot be used in this way unless the patient is agreeable.

What we would like to do is to use this channel we have found for writing, for helping doctors on the Earth Plane to come to the correct diagnosis of their patient's ills. We are working on this and, if it comes off, it will be a wonderful step forward. We are thinking about things all the time, over here. What we really need is more cooperation from those on the Earth Plane. If you think what could be achieved by consultation between your doctors and ours, for the benefit of the patient, it is very exciting. We know you have X rays and scanners to tell you what is the cause of the trouble but the treatment is left to the doctors concerned. What our doctors could do would be to give advice on how they see the condition from their point of view. This point of view, gathered from the spirit eye, could help your doctors come to a decision that would be absolutely right and also how to carry it out. This could be used in cases where you have complications. We think it is well worth a try and, as I say, we are working on it. Something else to worry our friend who is doing the writing. He wonders what we will say next.

Now the spirit doctors are usually those who have been doctors on the Earth Plane but they are very advanced and are of all nationalities. The West are not the only countries who produce fine medical men. The whole world does. But you do not hear much about them. There have been many healers on the Earth Plane who have had wonderful spirit doctors work through them and this will always be so, for, we over here are always on the lookout for channels that can be used for spirit work. This is very necessary for the life span for mediums on the Earth Plane is just as short as for others and as our work must go on we must have new channels coming along. If people would only look upon this work as normal we should have many more channels to work through but so many, who are sensitive, will not allow themselves to be used, for one reason or another, so there is nothing to be done. If it were considered normal to do this kind of work we would not be faced with the mental block that occurs. Then there are those who are afraid that they will be taken over. All this worry is needless. If you are sensitive and place yourself in our hands, no trouble can come to you at all. We see to that. It would be a fine way to repay you for your cooperation if we did not. No, whoever works with us will have their well being looked after. Have no fear of that. We can see quite a way ahead, you know, and in our best interest advice is given. What you do with it is up to you. You are all being helped by your guides, all the time. Some of the ideas that come into your head are put there. But always it is you who must act on what you are given. Sometimes, if we want something to happen to help us in our work, put a lot of pressure on the people concerned but, even then, the final word is theirs. If they do not want to do it, that is the end of the matter, we look somewhere else.

Those who are willing to work with us then tend to get overworked, the willing horse, but you can understand this for the more the channel is used it develops more and more and this, in turn, leads to others, over here, wanting to use it. If all agree, then away you go again, more work for that willing horse. But is is always in a good cause. We never waste time. Once the period of practice is over and the channel is fit to be used it is used at once and arrangements are made as to times etc. To fit in with the one on the Earth Plane who, after all, has its own life to lead and its clock to go by. As the channel is used more and more it becomes better and better at what it is doing and, in a way, this is its reward. The hours are still put in but the effort and concentration become less and therefore the work itself becomes easier. So that is that and I hope it will do some good for those who are interested and sensitive enough to be used. It is a very worthwhile job. Anything that brings the two sides of Life together is a help which can only bring joy to people. When people receive messages from their loved ones there is so much joy created on both sides. One good thing about the written message is that it can be read over and over by the one receiving it. Also it is easier to get the message across than verbally to some mediums. It takes longer and, of course, you cannot write in Church but we are thinking of other ways of using this kind of channel.

Do you wonder how this kind of writing takes place? I will try and explain. First of all we have to find someone on the Earth Plane who is a sensitive. Then that person has to agree to be used. After that the Spirit World must produce someone who will work with the Earth person. So far so good. The next thing is for the spirit person to be able to take control of the hand. They actually take the hand over in fact. They move in as it were. Then there is the spirit power which is harnessed to the hand and does the moving. It is this power which, at times, is hard to control. Certainly to begin with and that is why there is so much scribbling done. Then the spirit person learns to write all over again. This takes a lot of practice and frankly it can be very frustrating on both sides. Even today the power can be difficult but it can be burned off by scrubbing the hand on the table with a hand towel. This does the trick quite quickly. There is a point we would like to make here. We think that if you took a hand towel and scrubbed the table hard with it for about a minute and then wrote something at once the writing would not be very good. In our case the writing is steady and much improved. It is possible for the writing to take place without the Earth person knowing what is to be written but in this case we are able to give him the words and it helps. But the hand is moving without any effort on his part at all. He can stop at any time he likes but, once the pen is put to the paper, he relinquishes control and the spirit person gets on with the writing. Because of the power the writing changes from time to time, but you can see it is written by the same spirit person. This book is being copied, but messages can be dictated, and so far only one spirit person does the writing and we do not see this changing. I cannot tell you much more about this at the moment, so we will go on to the next subject.

Chapter 20

All the advice in the world will not help some people. They will go their own way and it is best to let them. If people are not prepared to listen; if they are always asking for more and more proof it means they are not ready to accept any proof at all, so you only waste your time and perhaps do harm if you force your thoughts upon them. It is better if they are left to come to terms with themselves first, then they will be more ready to listen. Many people come over without prior knowledge and they manage fine as long as they have an open mind and can accept their new situation. The main reason why we like people to be ready and understand about the new life they are going to is that it makes the home-coming far more enjoyable. Just as on Earth, if you want to get the best result from something you wish to do, you must find out all about it; make the right preparations for it, and so on. In this way the end result will be all you had hoped for. And so it is with your passing. The better prepared you are, the more you know about it, the more natural it will be and the more enjoyable. This applies equally to the ones left behind. As we have already said, if the whole business of passing can be treated as the natural thing it is; if the sadness can turn to joy, then it would be perfect. If people would only discuss death, as you call it, instead of treating it as a taboo subject, everybody would be much better off. Here we are, over here, alive and well and in the most beautiful surroundings. Happy and pain free, catching up with old friends, and enjoying ourselves as we cannot remember doing before, and there you are, on the Earth Plane, being miserable. It just does not make sense, now does it? We can go on and on about this for we feel so strongly about it. Happiness is not as you know it on Earth. It is the most perfect thing because it has love as its base. On the Earth Plane you have moments of happiness and you look back upon them wistfully, 'Ah, they were happy times', you say. Over here, happiness is the way of life, not moments but all the time. Once the grief and the pull of the Earth Plane is behind you, you are happy.

There is nothing to stop it except the thoughts that come from Earth. That is why it is so important for you people to understand this.

82

To us your thoughts are words to be heard loud and clear. There is a lot of truth in the saying, 'Do not speak ill of the dead', not, for the reason most people think, 'It is not the thing to do', but because your thoughts are heard by the person concerned and can give them a lot of pain. Maybe you are speaking the truth but it does hurt, and the person concerned cannot answer back. Thoughts are very difficult things to control and you are not expected to on the Earth Plane. People say 'I have my own thoughts on the matter'. And as long as they are not put into words you are all right. People say 'I was very careful what I said' and so on. You know all this. So now you must start learning to guard your thoughts just as you do your tongue. Thoughts find the person they are meant for. Please do not think that thoughts on the Earth Plane are heard over here by all. No, if this were so it would be like living at a football match all the time, or at an airport! We are spared this but thoughts are powerful things and they get through. We just say guard your thoughts in the same way as you guard your tongue and you will give no offence. Just keep the good thoughts flowing.

You must try to take it all in and we think you can. What we are trying to do is to paint you a word picture of what happens at passing, which can be accepted because it sounds right. If we gave you a picture which, to you, sounded way out, you would not be able to accept it. There is no point in doing this, so we have presented everything in a low key. If we started to tell you of the real wonder of this life then, with only your Earth life as a comparison, it would be too unnatural for you. You must therefore take what we have told you as fact. Only when you arrive here, will you realise that it is even more wonderful.

In the normal way we are not given much notice when a friend or loved one is due to pass over. Only in the case of disease can we see. Let me give you an example. A friend on the Earth Plane knows of someone who is unwell and they are worried about them. They talk about this to a medium or a sensitive. Then we over here receive the message, and are able to look into it. We see the sick person and talk to the Helpers who are with them. We can see the trouble for ourselves but we talk to the Helpers and they tell us what the true position is and we then pass this information to the friend on the Earth Plane. It takes very little time to do this and we are pleased to be able to help for it is further proof of the cooperation that can be achieved. We know if the sick one will get better and we know when they will not. Never be afraid to ask questions for if the answers we can give are helpful we are very glad and, as I say, we can gather our information very quickly. Help is what this life is all about. It is a wonderful thing. Everyone gets round to it sooner or later.

You may start off by saying that you had had a tough life on Earth, and are now going to sit back and enjoy this one, and you will, because that is what you want to do. But the time will come when the urge to do something will be upon you and it is then that you are ready to be used. What do you want to do? There are people ready to help you with your choice. You may have strong ideas about something, fine, if that is what you want to do, then you must. The thing is you must have training. You must become an expert, as it were, in the field of your choice. On the Earth Plane, the helper is very often an amateur who gives a service of some kind in their spare time. While this can be a help for some things, a lot of wrong information can also be given which may cause harm. You can see this. Here you are given training and are not allowed to do anything on your own, until you are ready. So much harm can be done by untrained helpers that every effort is made to see that this does not happen. In fact cannot happen. Here again the state of the soul, for the job, is plain to see. If there is the slightest sign of unreadiness then more training is given. Time means nothing, there are no 'exams' set and no pressure to pass them. When the soul is ready, all will know, and that will be the time for it to go to work.

We are asked about the correct method for healers to adopt on the Earth Plane. How they should go about it. This is not an easy one to answer. Different spirit healers have different methods. Generally speaking though the healer should start with a short prayer. He should ask God to allow His healing ways to pass through the hands of the healer, who is the instrument, into the part of the body that needs healing, and that your healing guides should draw near and arrange for God's divine Power to do this. He should ask for God's blessing on the healers and send love and thanks for all the help they are giving. That is enough to have the healing rays pass through the hands. You can ask for the healing in the name of Jesus Christ if you so wish. 'Whatsoever you ask in My name shall be granted unto you.' To which we say, Amen.

Do not think that all healing is arranged like that, you can ask for absent healing also. This is a very good method to use for helping those in need who will not agree to direct healing. Here the method used will vary with those asking for it, but you can again start by asking God to send His healing rays to the following people, each to their need, then give the names and, if known, what is wrong. It is not necessary to do this but if you know what the trouble is, it will be a help. If you hear that someone is better or improving always thank God for it. It is right that you should, also it helps with the love link that is between God and yourself. Never be afraid to ask for help and never forget to thank God for it. When you pray to God, when you talk to Him, when you ask for help, when you thank Him or, when you just think of Him, you are forging these links of love with Him and these links are very important for your soul. If you can make them strong on the Earth Plane you will be so much happier when you arrive over here. Here, we can never give enough praise to Him for what He has given us and done for us.

We always think it is said that so many on the Earth Plane find it hard to speak about God and His Son. Sad because they are missing so much by not thinking of Him who created us and without whom we would be nothing. There are times when Man's vanity leaves us speechless. Man thinks he has done it all and that God is someone to be spoken of on Sundays or perhaps Easter and Christmas. There are those who do not even think of Him then. Well, the time will come, and when it does, you, too, will be sad that you have cut yourself off from God for so long. We give thanks to God because we are now living as He would have us live. As in fact you on the Earth Plane would live if you were not so materially minded. If you were not so busy getting everything out of life, as you call it, material things that you really do not need, but must have. We could ask a lot of questions, for it was not long ago when we, too, were there and we know the non stop scramble that goes on to obtain enough money to buy these, by and large, unnecessary things. The battle leaves you exhausted but not happy. All so futile, and yet you hang on to life and fear 'death'. You hear of someone who has passed away and you think 'What a shame', 'So young', or 'He did not live long enough to enjoy this or that.' If only we had known half of what we know now, when we were on the Earth Plane, we would not have thought as you do. Hence this book.

Now what can we talk about? We have covered quite a few things but have we gone into them deeply enough? What we wish to emphasise more than anything is the state of the soul when it passes. Here is a subject that could make a book by itself. What is the soul? I have put that question to my teacher and he tells me that it is the spark of life that is given by God at the time you are first conceived. It is for this reason that abortion is wrong. We know this is going to upset many people, but there it is. The soul is the spark of life. Given by God, at the time of conception, and therefore abortion is murder. We know this point is debated on Earth by your medical profession. They say there is no life up to a certain time but they are wrong. The fact that they cannot detect it is beside the point. Life is there and it must not be taken. There are so many reasons man gives, for having abortions, and it is not our plan to debate them here. The point is that, as usual, man has a choice and if a child was not intended in the first place, it should not have been started. And as usual when man makes a mistake he then looks around for a way out. Do not doubt the truth of what we say. Our teacher assures us that we are absolutely right and that it has been needed to be said for a long time. There are plenty of people on earth who campaign against abortion, but the public think that theirs is just another opinion, without any stronger basis, than those who are for it under certain circumstances. Now you are being told the truth. Not an idea. Not an opinion. The truth. Abortion is murder. So the soul is the spark of life given by God at the time of conception. It grows as the body grows and from that very first moment it records everything that happens and it is the real you. Deep down, you know this is right. It also sounds right, so you should not have much trouble accepting it. Then again, at what other time could God give this spark of life? It has to be there from the very start for that is when the body starts to grow.

As the child grows, so the soul grows and records faithfully everything that happens to the child. Then on through youth and right through life. Always keeping the record, until the time comes to pass over when the soul is at last the person, the you, that stands revealed as the true you. On the Earth you talk about someone at last being seen in their true colours. You do not know how near the truth you are. The colour of the soul at passing is the true you at that time. We say at that time because, if the colour is unsatisfactory, then efforts must be made to have it changed. If that is the wish of the soul. Nothing can be done if the soul does not wish it. On the other hand if it does, there are helpers who will take the soul in hand and, with love and understanding help and guide it to full health. This is the judgement you hear about. It is you that decides what is to be done and you have to put up with whatever is necessary to achieve this. God loves you, but for your own good he arranges for you to do whatever is necessary to make your soul fit again, so that it can go forward. You caused your soul to be in the condition in which it arrived over here, and you will put it right. If you do not want to, that is up to you, but you cannot expect to be accepted by others if you do not fit into their way of spirit life. Having realised that you are sorry for the condition your soul is in, you repent. Then the Helpers can come to you and help you to ask for forgiveness. All will know if you are truly sorry, so we would not like you to think that your Earth Plane kind of sorry, that slips off the tongue so easily and means so little, will get you far here. No, you must truly be sorry so that it shows in your soul, before the cleansing process may start. If you doubt this, think for a minute. When you are really sorry for something you have done and you have faced up to it you feel much better about it don't you? Well, that is the soul, the real you. Just about to put things right with itself. Nothing can happen until you have faced up to the wrong you have done. Then you are given whatever help you need to put the matter right. Naturally there are always degrees of wrong.

And your idea of wrong and what our law says is wrong can differ. Your law and ours are both based on the ten Commandments. They tell you how you should behave. But you will remember that Jesus told the man Nicodemus who came by night: 'That a man should be born again before he could enter the Kingdom of Heaven.' And it is this that we are talking about. Before you can progress in the World of Spirit you must be cleansed of your Earthly sins and become as a new born baby as far as your soul is concerned. Now you will say: 'I thought we went to the Spirit World when we pass over.' Yes, so we do, but you remember that Jesus also said, 'In my Father's House are many Mansions.' Again He was telling the simple truth, for when you pass over you arrive at and stay in the most humble of these mansions. It is a very wonderful place this humble 'Mansion' and it will make you wonder what is to come if this is 'humble', but you must know that God wants the best for us always and He wants our souls to be in a fit state to enjoy it all. So we start off on this lowly Plane or Mansion and it is here that you make up your mind what to do. Remember, it is you who must take the first step. It is you who must feel that the time has now come to face up to yourself and it is you who must say that you repent and wish to start to put things right. You cannot start too soon, as far as we are concerned, and you do not have to wait until you arrive here, before you start either. Just remember, however, that it is between God and yourself. You can confess to anyone, if it makes you feel better, but there is no man who can forgive you. No one can, only God, and quite frankly, you have to be on this Plane before you can know if and when He has done this. The Confession makes you feel better but that is only the beginning, not the end of it, and the other thing is that you may have forgotten a lot of the things you need to ask forgiveness for. This is where the soul comes in. It has forgotten nothing. The real you knows it all.

All this information should not frighten you, it should make you feel glad that there is such a system that has your best interest at heart. You would be worried if it was left to the Earth Plane justice to do it instead. The simple fact of the matter is that whatever wrong you have done on the Earth Plane is recorded by the soul, but also the good, don't forget. It is not all bad ever. Your deeds, good and bad, colour your soul and it is this colour that must be perfect before you can advance to a higher plane. Whatever you have to do or suffer to put this right will depend on this colour. But you will have all the help you need to get you through this, and it will be given with love and understanding by helpers who wish you well. Who want you to succeed in this major task of yours. It is a major task, for it is the very start of your spiritual journey. Until this stage has been completed you cannot go on.

We will go on now to the question of belief. How you go about this will make a big difference as to how you lead your life on Earth, and therefore in what shape you arrive over here. Having been brought up in the Christian faith I can say now that it helped me. Others I have spoken to say the same thing but having said that I can tell you that other faiths have the same success or failure as Christians when it comes to preparing the souls of their followers for this life. Although Jesus, who is the Son of God, came to Earth and, during His short ministry, gave us much good advice as to how we should lead our lives and make ready for the next, not many people followed it. In this way our advantage has been lost. Much of the Christian teaching is in line with Judaism and so it should be, most of the early Christians were Jews and Jesus was born and brought up as a Jew. He quoted the Laws and the Prophets. But He wanted things changed so that all would understand the best way for people to know His Father and how to go through life as the Father wished. He wanted all to know that God loves them and that they should love one another. That the things of this world are as nothing compared to what is to come. Then again the different Muslim sects all worship God and we know that Mohammed studied the sayings of Jesus and used them in his teaching. We can go on, the Hindu and the Buddhist all have teaching that will lead them to God, if only they will follow them faithfully. But man being man thinks up clever little ways round the teaching of their spiritual leaders, and think they are getting away with it. But they do not. The crimes committed, in the name of religion, are crimes.

The terrible things that are done in His name do not please God at all. All slaughter just sickens us, over here, for we know, Christian and Muslim alike, that God does not like blood shed in His name and it must stop. He is grieved by so much that is done by the Churches of all faiths, in His name, and this fact is taught us over here, and that is why we try to get this message over to you. God is a God of Love. Killing must stop and that is that. So much that is done in the name of religion is seen by us over here to be silly. The simple teachings of the Leaders, given long ago, for reasons that were best for the people at that time, are carried on today and made part of religion itself. This is wrong and can be harmful for the soul if it is allowed to take hold of it. What you are made to believe on Earth, remains with you when you arrive here, and if these beliefs are strong enough the soul is crippled by them. This gives all concerned a lot of trouble to get the matter put right. You are what you are when you first arrive here and you can only change if you really want to. We cannot stress this enough. Do not think you change at all with passing. You are finished with your body, that is all.

We are now going on to the next question of what must be done with all this information we are giving you. You could of course forget it all. Or you could read each chapter again, and try to understand what it all means. Not that the message itself is difficult to understand from a language point of view, but perhaps it is from a practical point of view. You just cannot believe what we say, in other words. This is a great pity for we do not know how else to put it. Then perhaps you will say, 'All right I accept it'. If you do, and follow our advice, you will have a quiet life.

Chapter 21

What else can we tell you? Well, we have been asked to talk about our animal friends a little more. It seems that you want to know about their souls and do they advance in any way, in view of the service they give to man and the fine work they do?

The wonderful thing about the animal soul is that it is without sin, so their souls have nothing to answer for. You may think, the way some behave, they are full of it but chewed slippers do not constitute sin! And animals are not capable of it. They do not have the instinct that man has for doing evil. They have instinct that tells them what they should do to look after themselves, but not to use against others for their own ends. When wild animals kill others for food they do so for that reason only. Not for gain or exploitation. When a lion has made a kill it can walk through a herd from which it has just taken its prey and they will not run away. They know it will not need food again for a few days so they have nothing to fear.

Having been blind I am very interested in the Guide dog. They are wonderful and so are the people who train them. It is a big strain for both sides to achieve what they do. Despite what you may think, it is most unnatural for the dog to do this kind of work and he really is on tender hooks all the time. He understands that he has to look after the blind person but things are cropping up all the time and he is having to think about them and because it is not natural to him he is afraid he may do the wrong thing. On top of that he has no one, on the spot, to ask. Now most of these dogs are psychic. They can see and hear us in the spirit world, and the blind person's guide is with them most of the time, so they do receive some help. And the dog really does give over its life to the blind person.

Then you have those dogs that work sheep and cows. They work very hard also but it is more natural for them and they love it. They love being involved with the person they are working with and feel the importance of it all. We can go on but we have said enough to answer the question. The soul is without sin and therefore cannot change. It does not need a reward as far as that is concerned, but it does need all the thanks it can get and love also. This goes for all pets. Love and thanks and they are happy but also links are formed and you will never be parted from them. They will be waiting when you pass over.

Now for something else. Do you ever wonder how it is that some places seem familiar to you when you know that you have not been there before? The answer is that you have been there in your sleep. We have told you about Astral travel. The journeys the soul takes when the body is asleep. This happens with many people but because they do not remember they do not know about it. We meet our friends during this time and quite a lot is done for the soul, if that is what it wants, in the way of education. It is during this time that some of your problems are solved. Sometimes different possibilities are discussed and it may be thought that one thing should be done instead of another for the sake of experience or perhaps because in the long term it would be better. There is sometimes a lot more to your life than you think. But never fear, it is always with your best interest at heart. We will tell you of an experience we had, not long ago, during one of these visits.

We have a young friend whom I knew during my time on the Earth Plane. She was in a spiritual development circle that I belonged to and I thought she had the makings of a good medium. After I arrived over here I made a point of seeing if, in fact, I had been right about her. I am pleased to say I was, but I could see that she was far from happy with the way things were going for her. She felt that she was not getting on fast enough. This is a common fault with young people but once they feel like this it is hard to make them see sense. So we met over here and I was able to have a good talk to her. Being sensitive she was able to remember the gist of our talk, and she is now settling down and taking her time over the task of developing. Another time we were able to talk to a friend who unfortunately remembered nothing on waking. But all was not lost. He is very keen to get on and we are able to do his soul some good during these visits. Later he may remember, but anyway we are able to make him feel better. He is a great worrier, among other things, and we are able to show him that he has nothing to worry about and send him back to the Earth Plane happy. This happiness he remembers or feels when he wakes up. Now he cannot understand why he is happy instead of worried. What a man! You cannot win! There is so much we can do and it is a big pity that you cannot always remember. Nevertheless the soul does know and, as we say, much can be done for it, at this time, if that is what it wishes. It takes all sorts to make a world and it would not do for us all to be alike, but there are some who just cannot be given too much advice or instruction. They are at their chosen subjects all the time. Others are only to happy to sit back and enjoy the beautiful surroundings here.

I am often asked about Jesus. Have I seen Him, heard Him speak and so on? The answer to all that is 'Yes', I am happy to say I have. He is able to come down to this lower plane from the one He is on but we cannot go up to see Him. When He arrives there is always a big occasion made of it. He is greatly loved by all and no one misses a chance to hear Him speak. As I have already told you He is indeed the Son of God and therefore His word is listened to. In fact you could rightly say we hang on His every word. He teaches us very much as He did when on Earth. We have already taken the first step, but there are many more to take, and we must learn to develop our souls so that we will, one day, be ready to take the next one. What does He teach us? Love and service to others. The same simple lesson. The difference being that the degree of both becomes more refined over here and that is how it will always be. Love God and one another. Always help others to advance. This is something you should all be doing now. If you are not, then please do so. Time, as you know it, is running out. Everyone has such a short stay on Earth in real terms. You should be making the most of it. Do not doubt what I tell you. I am not writing this book for the fun of it, even if it does give me a lot of pleasure. I want to help you and all those you talk to on this subject. That has been my aim all along. Life, over here, is of such a fine quality that we want you to be able to appreciate it from the word go. The only way you can do this is to arrive in a fit and proper state. You would not visit friends in anything other than this, on the Earth Plane, so why not be the same when you greet your friends over here.

I know, you are asking, 'What about you, you who keep on about me?' I will tell you. I came over here in the normal way. That is to say my time on Earth was up and all arrangements had been made and were carried out. When I arrived over here with my Sister as guide and helper, I was in a state of exhaustion owing to my long and debilitating illness on Earth. It was necessary for me to have a good rest in one of our Homes. After that I found that my soul was in pretty good shape. Nothing to boast about, nothing to be ashamed of. How I had managed this, looking back over my record, I can only say was because I led a normal kind of life. I cannot go into that here although I know it is the kind of thing you want to know, so that you, yourself, will know what to expect. On the other hand, if you stop to think, most of us know the kind of people we are. We know that we have been silly, even stupid at times, but we have not been evil. We have been bad tempered at times and have said things we have regretted but they are passing things and do not damage the soul. Pushed too far, sometimes, we may do something back in spite. Most of the time we are sorry, even while we are doing it, and that kind of thing has little or no effect on the soul. Petty things you do not have to worry about and mostly that is all you have done. I remember writing to my wife, after I had been over here a little while, and telling her that as far as I could see all our friends would be all right when they came over. I had been to see them because, many I had not know before I became blind, and I wanted to see what they looked like. Of course, at the same time, I could see the colour of their souls and that is why I made that remark. For you then, we can say, do not worry about anything. The chances are your soul is in good shape and, if it is not, the big thing is for you to want it to be. Then, because it is God's wish and everyone else's you will be given all the help you need to achieve this. On top of that remember, once the soul has been restored to health, that is the end of it. No one points the finger as they do on the Earth Plane.

Those are happy thoughts for you to work on. *Do not worry, that is always our message.* We know only too well, from our own stay on the Earth Plane, that you do, at times, have real cause for worry. So much goes on over which you have no control and man's inhumanity to man is a terrible thing for us, over here, to witness. But, even so, it is limited to the Earth Plane and bad as that may be, it cannot go on for ever, as can the life you have before you over here. Take heart then and do not worry. We love to contact our loved ones and friends on the Earth Plane to give them messages of hope and good cheer but it is not easy for us. Some mediums are better than others but sometimes we cannot make ourselves understood to them. That is why this written word is so helpful. People have time, over here, to prepare their message and that is what is sent. And the message is there in writing and can be read over and over again. With a medium you sometimes cannot remember all that was said. Nevertheless the more contact that we can make the happier we are. So never be afraid to go to a medium, you are doing us both a power of good.

I have told you quite a lot now about my passing, for I believe that that is what you want to read about. Personal accounts are always easier to talk about anyway. The thing is to get the message over to you in the most acceptable way. Some people think that you know when you are going to pass over. In my case I can honestly say I did not. I got up as usual and felt as awful as usual. Had breakfast and carried out my usual chore of injecting myself with Insulin. Then my wife went shopping, which she would not have done if she had thought that anything was wrong. Friends called and we chatted. Everything, in fact, went normally that morning until my sister arrived. So what can I say other than that I was given not the slightest hint. Others I have spoken to, over here, have said the same thing. Sometimes people ill in hospital know that they are going, but we think that could be picked up from the nursing staff who know how ill you are. I have spoken to my Teacher about this and he says there is no warning system as such. Whatever knowledge we acquire must be from other sources. There is really no point in warning you. What good would that do and how much would you want? Most people have their affairs in order by the time they retire or earlier if they have children to consider. But that is not a consideration under the circumstances. As I have already said, when the time comes, off you go, you wait for nothing. We are given advice over here when we are personally interested, or if a friend on the Earth Plane is interested we can find out, but as usual the person involved is the last to know.

There is a great deal of talk these days on the Earth Plane of letting people die with dignity. This is because medicine has advanced so much in some directions and you now have life support machines and drugs that, as you say, keep people going. I am not too sure that doctors know what they are doing. If you have machines that take over the body functions so as to give an organ the chance to recover or a part to take over a part that has failed, well fine, but if the machine just keeps the body as a whole going there is no point. The soul will have left the body when its time has come, so all they are doing is keeping the body going. What is the point in that? As we have said before it is wrong to try and prevent death beyond a certain point. Doctors know pretty well what that point is, but rest assured, they do what they like about the body. But if the soul is ready to go then friends come for it and away it goes.

People who think they have died on the operating table or during a serious illness have, in fact, not done so. What has happened is that the soul has left the body, during the operation, in the same way that it does in sleep and has travelled as it always does, but in these cases they can remember their experiences. If the soul does not go too far away it can watch the operation and there is nothing odd in that. The Earth body cannot die as long as the soul is attached to the body by the cord. When the cord is broken then the soul has left the body for good and cannot go back. Well, so much for that for the moment. I could go on about it but really it would only be padding and we can do without that.

My big problem is to get the message over to you, so that you will accept it all. Not without question but after questioning. Question as much as you like, that is good for both of us. Question and answer is the way forward, but the questions must be considered thoughts, and the answers given must be full of logic, so that you are able to accept them. We can only anticipate your questions. The answers are supplied by our teachers, who would not be teachers if they were not highly qualified and highly evolved souls. Unlike the Earth Plane where teachers are young, out of teacher training colleges in the first place, with little or no practical experience, our teachers must have gathered great experience and learning before they are allowed to teach. The other way round to your ways. When you are taught something, over here, it is correct and may be taken as such. The questions we ask, for we have not been over here long, must be the kind of question you would ask for we are all of a like mind, at this stage. Everything that we have told you is correct, either coming from our teachers or having their blessing.

'Free Will' is a source of interest to us. What is it and why were we given it in the first place? We have mentioned it already but not too deeply. In the first place God has given us free will so that we may grow up as individuals and not as carbon copies of one another. We can therefore say, in a broad sense, that God has set us free to do what we like with our lives. But having done this He does not wash His hands of us. By His love He keeps hold of us, so that, come what may, we will return to Him. Battered about, maybe, by what our free will has got us into, on the Earth Plane, but again full of practical experience that has developed the soul so that it will be a worthy addition to the Group. There will always be the unfortunates who will allow their free will to take them too far. They will be punished for what they have done on the Earth Plane. And if the soul has been damaged in the process, it will have to be put right over here. Murder and suicide are the two crimes against the soul that give the most trouble for the soul is dispatched to the spirit world before its time. Without permission, if you like, and this upsets the system or cycle of spirit life. It does not matter if the state takes the life or a person does it, it is the same thing. God, with His love for us,

95

has arranged for the matter to be put right but He will not be mocked by man, and so the job of putting the matter right is not made easy. It is in the best interest of the soul that this is so. But remember there is nothing that cannot be put right for that is God's mercy and His love for us all. He shows this at every turn by the help that is given and the love and understanding that is shown to the sufferer. But suffer you must, for it is the only way that the soul may be cleansed if you have committed such a sin.

We cannot tell you of the suffering these poor souls go through, even if we wished to. That is a personal thing to the soul concerned. There is not a set punishment for this kind of thing as there is on the Earth Plane. Each soul must handle its own problem for itself. There are never two sets of circumstances the same, and remember, it is not punishment as such. The object of the exercise is to put the soul right, not to take revenge for what it has done. There is no society here who must be protected from these people. No prisons for them to be locked away in. It is just a matter for the soul and, when it is ready, the Helpers will be on hand to see the matter through. All corrective treatment of the soul must, by its nature and by necessity be unpleasant, and this is where the notion of punishment comes in. But it is not. Your child, after enjoying itself in the garden comes in happy but filthy to your living room. That starts things off, and the next thing is it finds itself in the bath. Now you think that you are getting it clean for its own good, but the child may think it is real punishment. This is a simple example that may get you thinking along the right lines.

We have all got something to answer for. It is not in the nature of Man for it to be otherwise. But mostly we can put ourselves right through service to others. The saying, that you can always find someone worse off than yourself, is a true one and the scope, over here, is limitless. So the opportunity for community service as we could call it, is there for you if that is what you wish. Now the help needed is spiritual. It is not a case of going shopping for someone or weeding their garden as it is with you. So it takes a lot of learning under the trained guidance of a Helper. You see, the one being helped has asked for it. If they sense that the person helping does not know what they are up to they may reject the help and perhaps not ask again. Remember they have free will, and this could set their development back, to their disadvantage, and therefor to the disadvantage of the Helper. Success is the thing that counts, for that means progress. So the important thing for the Helper is to gain the complete confidence of the one needing help, and you can only do that by knowing your job.

As I have said before Helpers are usually ones who have suffered themselves and know what it is all about. They are able to bring love and understanding to those they are working with. There are never two cases the same but the understanding of the problem is there. Helpers are chosen for cases, the more difficult ones going to the more experienced and the degree of the help needed is ascertained from the colour of the soul. Once a Helper has been given a case, as it were, they stay with them until the cure is complete. If they feel, at any time, that they need advice or help then there are more advanced Helpers available to them. The experience of these Helpers, after so many cases, is of a very high order, as you can imagine.

We must never forget the choice we have in everything. It is not always best for us to win everything and be absolutly right every time. You see, we must live in a world with other people who are not always as strong as we are and, quite frankly, are unable to accept that they are in the wrong. When this happens it is in the best interest of all if the strong ones give way. They are big enough to do it and they should. Do you see the point of this? Good. Always make allowances for our weaker brothers and sisters. God loves them, with all their faults, and so must we. Having made that point we will call the matter closed and move on.

Chapter 22

Never doubt that God loves us all. You find this word Love difficult to handle and this is understandable, for it has been debased on the Earth Plane, by many, for what it conjures up in the human mind. The love God has for us is all caring. He will have us happy and healthy. Free from all the things that spoil the quality of your life on Earth. When you arrive here, as I have said many times before, you are what you were on Earth but without your Earth body to hide your true feelings in. This can give you a bad time if your nature is one of greed, jealousy or deceit etc. For this will be plain for all to see. Now these things can be overcome on the Earth Plane by discipline. After all you are just giving way to base feelings. It is not always easy to do this, especially if people, who seem much better off all round than you, are for ever being pushed before you on television or in papers and magazines. But, however hard it is, you must overcome all such base feelings, for they have no place over here at all, and if you have not overcome them then you will find it impossible to live with others here and will find yourself instead living with like-minded people. Not a very cheerful prospect and one that you will have to work hard to escape from. In fact until all these negative thoughts are cleansed from the soul, you will not. Nothing is easy. Everything worth while must be worked for and it is usually hard.

While you are on the Earth Plane you should work hard on the nine Beatitudes that Jesus gave you, for he knew exactly what He was saying when He said 'Blessed are the pure in heart for they shall see God. Blessed are the meek for they shall inherit the Earth', etc. Look them up in your Bible (Matthew 5.1.12) and take them to heart for they will stand you in good stead when you arrive here. Read about Lazarus who sat at the gate day after day begging (Luke 6.19.31). You do not have to be a begger to learn what he did. Just make sure that you arrive here in a condition that will allow you to live comfortably with others. If you do you will be happy. If you do not you will have your happiness deferred for a time until you can. If only people would be satisfied with what they have. If only they would realise that their time on Earth is short and they are just wasting their time chasing after worthless material things when they could be preparing for the real happiness ahead. Then they would be doing something worth while indeed.

We never know when our hour will come. Jesus taught this and told His followers to pray and be prepared (Matthew 24.42). When we are young passing into spirit never enters our heads and good care is taken by all to see that it does not. From here we cannot see why this should be. If the business of death is discussed properly then there is no reason why the young should not be instructed, for their own good, from as early an age as possible. But we fear that the grown ups, by and large, are not in the right frame of mind themselves to do this. Until death is treated as just another step forward, in our long, long journey to God, it will not be treated as the normal thing it is. People talk about 'from the cradle to the grave' in the same light as they would say 'from start to finish' or 'beginning to the end'. If people go on being encouraged to have this outlook, then it will be hard to make progress. I was speaking to a little boy, only the other day, who had just passed over. He was rather bewildered as you can guess. It seems he came over as the result of a car accident. One minute he was a happy child with his people on Earth, the next he was over here. In cases like this there are Helpers who step in and look after these young souls until they have settled down and relations come along and take them home with them. This is fine and works well, but the young one misses his people, just as they miss him, and there is a lot of misery all round. If this young soul had been told about death, and knew enough about it to accept his new situation, it would have been much better for all concerned. Also the parents would feel much easier about it if they knew how well their son was being looked after. In cases where two or more of the family come over together, as the result of an accident, it is wonderful to see how quickly they settle down and how happy they are. So much could be done if only the right education was available on the Earth Plane.

Perhaps this book will start something. We think it will. We think most people are crying out for something like this. Something they can believe. In many ways I am sorry I was not a public figure. If I had been well known I could make myself known to people and perhaps they would find it easier to accept me and what I say. Unfortunately that is not the case. I was and am, known to quite a few people, but they are in the Spiritualist Movement, in the main, so I am preaching to the converted. Many of them, if they read this book, will know it is I who am writing it and that will help them, but for the rest of you I hope it will be a case of 'truth will out'. For the truth it is and indeed what would be the point of writing it if this was not so? I am not an author writing a book for sale on the Earth Plane. You will have to pay for the book, yes, but I do not need the money and nor does my friend through whom it is being written. So you see the prime motive is to get the truth across to as many people as possible who will read it. I would be less than honest if I did not tell you that my wife, who is still on the Earth Plane, stands to gain from this book. I am afraid I did not provide too well for her during the time we were married and then the last years of my blindness were a drain on what we had. So you see I can do something for her whilst I am doing something for you. When I come to think of it, there cannot be many husbands who have provided for their wives in this way, in fact I may be the first, so on top of everything else history is being made. This book could be making history. Enough of that, let us think of something else that will interest you.

Chapter 23

We will talk about messages, sent from Spirit, to loved ones on the Earth Plane. These can be very wonderful for both the sender and receiver. Especially if the one receiving can accept it. The one in spirit prepares whatever it is they want to say, just as you gather your thoughts before writing a letter, but after that, things change according to the method used for sending it. If you go to a good medium the chances are the loved one will come through and speak to you, but it may not be too successful for it is not easy for them to do so, and they may not be able to stay very long. Or the loved one may be able to pass the message through the medium rather than directly. Again, much will depend upon the medium and how well the message is relayed. In all cases there must be help and understanding on both sides. It is not always easy for the message to be sent and not always easy to accept. The best method of all is automatic writing for both sides are able to prepare what they have to say, questions can be asked and answers can be given, and it is all in writing. The only snag is, it is slow, and there is not the personal touch that you have with the voice.

Many people are disappointed, after a sitting, because they expected too much. You know by now that the one departed is exactly the same but without the body. They have not gained any magic powers except to see rather more into the future than you can and the real state of health of people, but apart from that they are very much the same. So do not expect them to be able to solve your problems more easily now than they could before. If their advice was good before it will be sharper now, for from here, they can see more sides to the problem and also they know the thoughts of others and may get the end picture. But if they were just good at keeping pigeons, then they still are, and will not be able to advise you on the state of the Stock Market. If they were never very good at remembering dates and that kind of thing, they will be the same. But because they are often with you they know what you are thinking and can therefore tell you what is in your mind. In other words they remember if you tell them, just as you did on Earth.

But if you can find someone who can write, you can start a correspondence that can be very rewarding. You can ask qeustions and, given a little time, the answers will come back. We always advise people to write their questions down. Keep them to the point and do not make a question a double sided one. Then number them. If you do this and keep the questions with you, you will receive your answers and will know exactly what you have asked. We can write answers to verbal questions but we find the person asking the question does not always remember what was asked. If there is a Yes or No on the page it can be tricky. Whichever way you use for contacting your loved ones, you should do so with love and understanding and always remember it is not that easy for them to come through. If you keep on asking for more and more proof, and that you really are speaking to the person they say they are, can prove to be very tiresome. Accept the proof they can give and don't ask too much. On the other hand they are only too keen to prove themselves. If you listen carefully and read, you usually pick up the personality of the loved one but for that you must be sympathetic.

There are other ways of contacting the departed souls but, unless you have very strong guides over here, we do not recommend these methods. You leave yourself open to be contacted by Earthbound spirits who can be mischievous and, at times, most unpleasant. We cannot think of anything else useful to you on that subject. But perhaps we should mention the mediums. Some are much better than others and all have off days. Do not always expect too much and if you can find the written word, so much the better. If only all this could be treated as natural so much more could be done. There are so many potential mediums about who do not know it because they would not dream of going to spiritualist meetings to find out. Then there is the doubt in the minds of some sensitives that a message, if sent, will not be accepted and because of the attitude of people towards this, trouble can be caused. Why in this day and age should people be made to feel like this? Why is it that this wonderful linking of the two worlds should be looked upon by so many as the work of the devil? We are sorry to say it, but it is sheer ignorance on the part of many and compounded by the teaching of your religious leaders. They teach you that Jesus appeared to His disciples after he had been killed on the Cross, to prove that there was no death; that He spoke to them and filled them with joy, even doubting Thomas was won over. They teach all that, but when it comes to others confirming what Jesus said and did to be true, they say it is the work of the devil. We admit things have improved. Mediums are not thought mad or burned at the stake these days, but after all these years Christian thinking has not changed very much. And yet we know that people, all over the world, are crying out to be told the truth but it is being withheld. Why?

The Church has investigated Spiritualism, as they call it, but the findings were never made public. The short answer being, that they found nothing but good in it, and were afraid of what would happen to the Church if they acknowledged it. Their power over people, such as it is, would be eroded even further. That is the truth and it is up to you to make your own way towards the light by seeking. What a difference it would make if the whole World were taught that there is no death; that life goes on and, if you wanted, you could go to Church three times a day, and have it proved to you. Don't you think that that kind of teaching would improve the quality of life on Earth? Don't you think people would spend more time getting their soul in good order for the next world instead, as they do now, of spending so much time on material things because they have been left in doubt as to whether there is anything after this, as they put it. it is not good enough that people's souls should be so badly advised. That they should be left to themselves to stagger about in the dark, on their own. They have free will and they exercise it by not going to Church. This is all wrong, they should be going to Church to be told the truth, not to take part in a ritual, the greater part of which means nothing to them. if their favourite hymns are sung they are in luck, after that we believe your Church goers would be hard pressed to tell you what the sermon was about a few hours later. All this, from where we are, seems to be such an awful waste of time. Your Earth life is short enough but when so much time is taken up in filling the soul with bad habits and wrong thinking, it seems such a terrible thing, a terrible waste. And it all has to be put right, over here, which is a further waste of your time, to put it mildly. Talk to people over here and they all say the same thing, they wish they had made better use of their time on Earth and they wish their teaching had been more enlightened.

We have now to consider, what you might call the next piece of advice that we have for would-be-champion-souls in training for the next world. Easy enough to say, difficult enough to carry out. Most things you like, on the Earth Plane, are bad for you. But you know that already without me telling you. All who think they have a sudden change for the better, when they die, are in for a bit of a shock. By now you will know that there is no change. All your habits, good and bad, come with you. So if you are keen to do better by your soul, having read this far, then you should start to get rid of all your material habits such as smoking, drinking and over eating. Also self discipline is a very useful thing to arrive over here with. The amount of free will you enjoy makes this very necessary. Never think for a moment that life over here is one long holiday or party. People are happy and go about their occupations with joy, but all work at something, once they have settled in. 'What about that free will', you say, 'if I want to sit around doing nothing I will'. So you can, but you will realise that sitting around doing nothing is not half such fun as joining others doing something. So after a while you will ask what you can do to be of help. Working over here, is a pleasure. Unlike on the Earth Plane where it so rarely is. Then again we have our leisure time and our sport. So, in this way we enjoy everything over here, which should make the effort needed to get your soul fit so much easier.

People think that drinking is bad for the soul. We do not know how this idea came about. It is not. Bad for the body if you go on drinking too much for too long, but not the soul. What is bad about drinking besides the social evils, is if it takes you into places where Earth bound spirits hang around. Here the danger is that unless you are strong spiritually or have strong guides, these Earth spirits can attach themselves to you, and introduce thoughts to your mind that are not in your best interest. Many a one has finished up in trouble because of this kind of thing. Most of the time it is put down to drink, but frequently it is more than that, and at times it can be dangerous. When you arrive here with a craving for alcohol there is no way you are going to find any to help you, so if you do not want to give yourself a bad time, be free of the craving before you arrive. Never doubt that this is so. Before we go any further with this subject let me say that I have nothing against drink. I had more than my fair share, when I was over there where you are, and that has not harmed me at all. It is just that, if you bring a craving of any kind with you from Earth, you are not going to be able to satisfy it here and are therefore going to have a bad time getting over it. That is the message.

We can now talk of life, over here, once you have settled. Yes, we have written about this already, but it is a big subject, and we can talk of different things. We know that personal experiences are always of interest so, as the most natural thing for me, I will talk about myself and what I get up to. Much of my time is taken up with this book. Not only thinking what to say but discussing with my sister and friends how best to put it over. Then I have had to take advice from my teacher. Nothing what I get up to. Much of my time is taken up with this book. Not only thinking what to say but discussing with my sister and friends how best must go into this book that is not basically true. This is important, for no word at all from us is better than an untrue or false one. We must be very careful not to give anyone on the Earth Plane the chance to prove this book to be wrong. As it is, we are going to have a lot of people speak against it. They are going to say that it is all in the mind of my friend who is doing the writing. Naturally, anyone can say that, but when the time comes we shall be able to prove that this is not so. In fact we look forward to the time when this happens, for we have all our helpers lined up behind us to see that the truth wins in the end, as it must. And those who speak against the book are going to have a few surprises coming their way and will have to eat their words. We say this in a spirit of fun for we know that people, who do not understand how this book is written, will be open to enlightenment. We must have opposition, so that we can make our proof the stronger. As I say, we are looking forward to putting our wits against all comers, it is going to be fun and it will do our case a lot of good. The more we can get people talking, the better.

After working on the book and all the things that go with it, I may go for a swim. I love swimming here, it is soothing and restful and it is so good for you. Water plays a big part in healing over here. It is the same on the Earth Plane, which is why most people love being near water although they really do not know why. Very few can go past water of any kind without looking at it, be it pond, river, or stream and they sit by the sea for their holidays. So I swim or go for a walk. We have beautiful walks here. Through woods along the bank of a river or stream. Over the hills I told you about. So many walks and always the wild life to entertain you. Not shy as on Earth, but happy and playful as only some of them know how to be.

Then I must visit my wife and friends who are still battling it out on Earth. I can make my presence known quite well to some. This, my teacher tells me, will pass with time but while it lasts it is a good feeling. Some I can talk to through the board, and I am asked plenty of questions which is good for both of us. It keeps the link strong. No doubt the ouija board in this case is somehow safeguarded but it is not recommended for general use. In fact it can be dangerous. Then, of late, I have had people over here wanting to use my friend, who is doing the writing, to write messages for them, to their loved ones. This is turning into quite a business for we have to decide who really needs the message sent; how urgent is it and so on. Not least is the question, will the person on Earth accept it? One case the other day was such a one. Having looked into all the angles it was decided the message could be sent. We were right, we are pleased to say for we now know that the message was well received and much joy will be brought to all concerned as the questions and answers gather pace. It is a big step to take for some people, writing about spirit matters, for it is never known how it will be received. I speak of people on the Earth Plane, not us. We knew it would be all right, our friend did not. Now he does, and he will trust us in future and not keep on asking if we are sure it will be all right. That is the Earth Plane for you, no one has too much faith. In fact we would not ask him to pass on a message if it was going to cause trouble, there would be no point, but we knew how he felt. So we have started on a new venture even before the book is finished. This is a good thing for we will keep our hand in, in this way, and it will bring much joy to all and you cannot have too much of that. Already my writing friend is a different man and that is as it should be. He has been through the fire with all his practice, now for the reward. He will share in the joy the messages he writes will produce. Already he has had some experience of this, so he knows what is to come.

Never doubt that an act of kindness or help, shown between you on the Earth Plane and those in spirit, goes without notice. It is the most wonderful thing for us to know that we can keep in touch with our friends and loved ones once we have passed over. The knowledge that we can still be of help when so many think we have gone for good, gives us a wonderful feeling of still belonging. And this keeps the link between us strong. So instead of letting the dead sleep, as some quaint saying goes, you should make every effort to keep in touch. Do not think of them as being dead but on the end of a telephone. If you can go on thinking of the one departed as being very much alive this will help them to settle down over here and in time your reunion will be between loved ones, as remembered, and not as strangers.

We have heard it said 'I wonder why old so and so has not come through to talk to us.' This from people who go to Church and sit listening to others receiving messages. Perhaps I should explain that during a Spritualist Church meeting, time is set aside for the medium to give a demonstration of clairvoyance and clairaudience. Messages will be received and given to members of the congregation. Usually they are messages of love and hope, given when it is needed, to those who are in need of help during a bad time in their lives. There are plenty of such people on the Earth Plane. You pass them by without noticing, because unless they can show how they feel by signs of distress you cannot know and most people do their best to hide their true feelings anyway. But for us it is easy. We know from the colour of the aura exactly what is wrong. Now the Church will be packed with spirit friends and they would like to make themselves known to you, each and everyone, but the spirit guide who helps the medium, will make sure that the people who are really in need of messages receives them. This is only right as you will agree.

The point I am making here is, do not think your friends have forgotten you or cannot be bothered to make the effort. If the chance is given to them, they will take it, but until then go on thinking about them and keep your friendship links strong for the time which must come when you will meet again. It is such a pity that the whole world cannot be made to see that the departed one lives on. The vast amount of useless harmful suffering that is going on all the time, would cease. It is completely negative and if you could see it, rising up as an ugly black cloud from Earth, you would be as horrified as we are. The passing of a friend or loved one should be a time of great joy. We have said it before but we cannot get it over too strongly, for most people on Earth do not want to listen. It is a fact, there are those who just will not listen and there are those that are all ears. When Jesus told someone to follow Him, the man asked time to go home to bury someone who had just died. Jesus said, 'Let the dead bury their dead.' As usual He had hit the matter right on the head. The dead should bury the dead. If you try to speak to such people and they will not listen then it is best to leave them alone. The Bible is full of cases where people would not believe but also full of cases where they did. You know them if you know your Bible. The woman, a Canaanite (Matthew 15.21.28) who even amazed Jesus, and the one who touched the hem of His robe, and was cured (Matthew 9.20.22). Such faith have some and they are indeed the blessed ones. But while we say do not press the one who will not believe we do not mean that we should just forget them.

Pray for them. Ask that they be given understanding and that the light of truth may enter into their darkness. Prayers are powerful things and should be encouraged in every way, for, just as your thoughts for departed friends keep strong the links between you, your prayers make your link with God. So talk to Him as much as you can and think of Him. Not just when you need help but also when you are happy. Thank Him for everything and mean it, for everything comes from Him in the first place. You should understand this, and accept it for it is the truth. Without God we are nothing. On the Earth Plane we think that all we have is made by man and that our thanks are to him. Your scientists are now coming to realize that this thinking is wrong. If God had not given us the wherewithal in the first instance we should have done nothing on the Earth Plane at all. In fact Man in his slap happy wasteful way is fast using up his natural resources in the most frightening fashion. Soon you will be in a sorry mess and to whom will you turn then? Let us finish on a cheerful note. There is no such thing as a non believer. All will believe in time, only some are quicker at it than others. It is God's wish, and you should know by now that His Will rules over here.

On, on we go, giving you lots of good advice we hope you are going to take. But like taking the horse to water, it is up to you if you drink or not. We hope you will say. 'He must be right, he would not just make all that up.' And you are right, as bright as I think I am, I must say I am not bright enough to think of all this. That goes for my writing friend as well. Between us, and all our friends, who are helping over here, we are bringing you the truth, pure and simple. We are, as they say, telling it as it really is, and for you and us that cannot be a bad thing. Be happy, the troubles of the Earth Plane we know can be bad, but think what is to come when you pass over. Spend as much time as you can in prayer. This will help you. Not on your knees, but talk to God as you would to the friend He is. Much that has you worried will never happen. Try to be happy as far as you can. It is good for your soul. If you are always sad and miserable it has a bad effect upon it and this can become a habit just as much as drinking or smoking. Happiness is the best habit of all, so try to cultivate it. Bless you.

And now what about your approach to life, is that of interest? Most people when asked say they do not have one, they live from day to day and they find this is enough. Some are ambitious, they want to get on they say. Well it takes all sorts to make a world. What we never seem to hear about is what people are doing about their spiritual life. If we say, 'come on, what are you going to do?', we are either told, 'nothing', or 'mind your own business'. Now the reason you are on Earth, in the first place, is because of your spiritual life, which is to do with the development of your soul. So why not do something about it? If you ask why people are on Earth at all you will not receive an answer. People do not think about it, or if they do, do not come up with the right one. Life is a school from start to finish. We must make the most of its teachings if we are to get on in our lives to come. Half the time, this aspect is not even considered by the masses, and, who is there among them, to pull them up short? Make them think of what they are all about. No one tried to get hold of me when I was one of the masses. I was left to stumble into the spiritualist movement on my own, more or less. Once I was given this kind of teaching, I never looked back. It changed my life. Now don't you think there could be countless others like me, who wish they could stumble into the truth, and have their lives changed as mine was? Yes. But why should such an important thing in your life be left to chance. Of course in many ways it is not. You are pushed by your spirit guides towards the truth and if you have ears to hear then you hear, but again, you have a choice, and you may hear but decide to do nothing about it. Pity.

I can remember, so well, the pleasure I always got from talking about spiritualism with my friends. Some were knowledgeable, some were not, but just to sit and talk did something to me. I loved it. Why this should be I cannot say but I do know that it is the same with most spiritualists when they are together. Talk will get round to this subject and the chances are that is where it will stay. Do other religious sects do this, I wonder? Anyway we do not think that Christians are much given to this, and yet they should be for they are followers of Christ. Christ who came to Earth to teach us. Who suffered so much and whose short life is such a marvellous story. Christ the Son of God, who did so much for us and yet we never talk about Him to our friends. Never recount with joy the things He did for mankind during the time He was on Earth. At Christmas we celebrate His birth, and what a way we do it! At Easter we think of His death. That is about all. We really do not deserve Him. But He is always there if we do want Him. How can we make the world believe

109

that there is no death, that life goes on, if, after all he did and suffered for us, we will not believe Him. We really must go further into this.

God sent His Son to Earth, for at that time the world was in a mess. Much worse than it is today, but I speak of a spiritual mess not material. In those days there were gods for everything and each nation had its own. The Jews knew the truth, for they worshipped God from the start. This I know because my teacher has told me so. The Jews, being the true believers, were indeed the chosen race. God hoped that He could build upon this belief so He sent His Son Jesus among them to do that. Well, we know what became of Him. God's trust in the Jews was misplaced, and that is a terrible thing to have to say, but He knew that having given Jesus to them. He had to let them choose how they would behave. There would have been no point in sending Him otherwise. Now we know what Jesus achieved in such a short time. His teaching has gone round the world and, when you think what the teaching was before Him, you must accept that the world is in much better shape now than then. Most people now acknowledge one God and only one which is a very big step forward.

Much of this book complains about the lack of preparation that is given to the soul on Earth, and it makes us very sad to see the missed opportunities that man does not take. After all that Jesus taught him. Looked at in the broader sense, the improvement in Man's thinking since Jesus is enormous. An in this light we are told, by our teachers, that God is well pleased. The fact that the Jews would not accept Jesus was a great disappointment to Him but in other ways He was a success. And remember not all the Jews rejected Him. It was in fact quite a near thing whether He was accepted or not. It was only the hard core that would not for personal reasons, although they turned them into religious ones. Jesus had to challenge their teachings, for the truth was being polluted by them, and therefore the people's souls were being put in danger. We know that if they had chosen wisely all would have been well. They had the same choice as Saul of Tarsus. You all know the story of his conversion on the road to Damascus. Strongly against Christ as he was yet, after Jesus spoke to him, no one could have changed round and done more for Christianity than he. He had his choice. It was brought home to him that all his religious fervour was misplaced, and he had the wit to see it. We know that his encounter with Jesus was dramatic but remember Saul was a strong character, fervid in his religious beliefs and he was most single minded when it came to the persecution of Christians. He was at the stoning to death of the first Christian martyr St. Stephen, But he accepted Jesus so totally that his life was in danger from the Jews, and he was naturally heartily distrusted by the Christians. Nevertheless, and despite all this, he travelled far and wide preaching the word that Jesus had given to all. He suffered as few other men have suffered, for his faith. Remember he could have led a comfortable life, if he had gone on as he was before he accepted Jesus. But no, he travelled all over the Mediterranean countries in great poverty, was beaten countless times for his teaching and was frequently jailed. All this suffering he accepted with joy because he was doing it for God and Jesus. If this one devout Jew could do all this, what a pity the others at that time, could not. If they had, life as you know it would have been very different. We could go on writing about St. Paul for he was such a fine man in the truest sense, but you can read about him yourself. There are plenty of good books about his life, and his work is written up in the Bible. The point I want to make is that the Jews, like everyone else, had free will and they chose the wrong way. Some of them that is to say. God could have saved Jesus at any time. Jesus Himself could have done so. He had free will as well remember, but He knew that if He did, all His teaching would have been in vain and that the plan God had made to help man would have failed. So He was killed on the Cross and then appeared to His friends and followers so that they could preach the simple truth that there is no death.

He also appeared to Paul, and the Gentiles were given their teacher, as Simon saw so plainly when Jesus was taken at an early age to the temple by Mary and Joseph to be registered; he was deemed to belong to the Lord, being their first born male child. He was also to be 'the Glory of thy People Israel' and so He was, but they chose not to see it. Many Jews became Christians in those days, so all was not lost and many become Christians today, but it is not until they arrive over here, that they realize how they were led astray in those early days, and how they are still led astray today. If the whole world had accepted Christ, and His teaching, what a happy place it would be. You can see this for yourself. Man has made so much trouble by his unChrist-like actions. History is full of it. History is the record of Man's failure to listen to God. Then, when man comes face to face with his own folly he wants to know why God allows it to happen. Men fight wars and each says God is on their side. The atheist points to all this and says there cannot be a God. All because Man would not listen to God and His Son Jesus

Christ. But it is never too late. You can become another Simon in the temple or an Anna, if you wish. They both recognized God in that Child, St. Luke (2.21.40) in your Bible. For me, as for others, it is a very beautiful story and one that should be taught more often than it is. If I had my way, every child would be taught it so that they would know that from the very start there were some devout Jews who accepted Jesus as being the Son of God. As I have said before, I am not a religious teacher nor even a lay preacher, but I have listened to my teacher over here, so I do know what I am talking about.

We are very fortunate to have such teachers. If you show an interest in any subject, you will be given the opportunity to study it with the best there is in that field. Knowledge can be such a hit and miss thing on the Earth Plane. I do not speak of higher education but of the average school. Then again, very few people bother to go on learning, once they have left school, and this is a pity for there are some who can learn much more easily when they are older. Anyway, when you arrive here you will be able to go on learning if you wish. If you are interested in the Life and Times of Jesus, then you can have the truth about everything that happened during that time, and much of it you can hear from the Master Himself. He is only too willing to instruct us. When He arrives we are called to the arena where, you will remember, we had the Healing Service for the spiritually disabled. Then He will lecture us on the different aspects of His time on Earth. It is always a very wonderful experience for us to listen to Him. The first time one hears Him is perhaps the most impressive and almost impossible to believe. He stands there clothed in the most beautiful colours you have ever seen. I know you are finding this extremely difficult to take in and, in your place, I would feel the same, but it is but the truth and you will have to accept it as fact, like so much else we have told you.

The last time He spoke to us it was upon the Crucifixion. He said that the event was very much as reported in the Bible. He said that he had known for some time that it was going to happen and there was nothing to be done about it. He could not have side-stepped it, once the officers of the Temple had made their choice. When the time came it was a sense a relief for He knew it would soon be over even if those hours were to be so terrible. He said the heat of the day was extreme and also flies plagued Him, being attracted by the blood on His head and face. This does not appear in the Bible. Jesus says that He did not say: 'My God, My God, why hast thou forsaken me?' as stated in one

112

account. He says He had no reason to say this for He was fully supported by God during the whole of His mission on Earth. The other thing He wanted to make clear was that He was very happy on Earth. This does not come over well in the Bible, but the fact was that He was exalted for much of the time, being filled with the Holy Spirit. He did find the going hard at times, being human accounted for this, but never for long. Once He had been recharged, He could go on again. We have already said that you would find this difficult to believe but take courage, it is all true. We will never ask you to believe anything that is not. When Jesus addresses us it is always fully attended, for He has such a wonderful presence. People felt this on Earth, over here it is even more pronounced. No one else can say things the way He can. Just sitting looking at Him is a joy but when He speaks he makes the situation He is talking about come alive for us. We could sit and listen for ever.

We have spoken a lot about Jesus and we wish people on the Earth Plane would do the same. We think it is wrong that so many children go through school without being taught the Bible. We know that schools are mixed, these days, but that is not a good enough excuse for keeping so many children in ignorance. Surely man can think of a way round that. If the child does not receive religious instruction at school, and does not go to church, what chance does it stand when it grows up? This is really dreadful seen from here. The stories in the Bible, told correctly and explained properly can catch the imagination of young people and help them on their way through life. That in turn means that they will arrive over here, in due course, in much better shape. It is the responsibility of all, parents, teachers and friends as well, to see to it that the word is passed along. God sent Jesus to teach us that there is no death, that we live on and He gave us a set of rules to live by so that we should arrive in the Spirit World in the best possible condition. How can man be so stupid as to do nothing about it? Will he never face up to what is ahead of him. Will he always wring his hands and say 'If only someone had told me'. Well, we are telling you. So you had better not be one to wring your hands when you arrive. We do not think it a bad idea to get tough about this at times. You see, when Man arrives over here, and in trouble, it is the Helper who must work so hard to help put the soul straight. Man must suffer but no one enjoys that. Far better to arrive trouble free.

We are nearing the end of this book. We have enjoyed writing it and if we have made a few people think it will all have been worth while. It is important, we think, to finish with something that will really grip you and can be easily remembered.

> The life that I have
> Is all that I have,
> And the life that I have
> Is yours.
>
> The love that I have
> Of the life that I have
> Is yours and yours and yours.
>
> A sleep I shall have,
> A rest I shall have,
> Yet death will be but a pause:
>
> For the peace of my years,
> In the long green grass
> Will be yours and yours and yours.

I loved these words. Perhaps you will. It really sums up what our life over here is all about. Love. Loving God and one another. If you have love in your heart you are all set up for life over here. Mark you, conditions are so much better for your thoughts here than on Earth. You do not have the pressures of your modern living to contend with. But having said that, the quality of life is so much better you have to try harder yourself. In other words, everyone moves up market a bit over here, if you will accept the expression. Please pass this book on when you have finished it and, if you want to, talk about it with others. We must get people thinking the right way, and the only way to do that is to think and talk about it until the whole question of passing over becomes natural to you. No fear, no pain and a dear friend to meet you. God Bless you.